Praise for *The Road Trip That Changed the World*

Mark Sayers is one of the most important thinkers in the church today. This book is filled with his typical insights and genius in answering the question of why the church is struggling today. You will be informed, inspired, renewed, and compelled to recover a serious, Jesus-centered discipleship and hunger for the Kingdom of God. Highly recommended.

  —**JON TYSON, PASTOR,** Triniᵗʸ ᴳʳᵃᶜᵉ ᶜʰᵘʳᶜʰ, ᴺᵉʷ ʸᵒʳᵏ & ᶜⁱᵗʸ ᶜᵒˡˡective

In this masterfully written book, our fri[...]ed the cultural code of millions of young adults. His[...]e psyche, and of spirituality sometimes border on th[...]akes his place as a major prophetic voice to the con[...]

  —**ALAN AND DEBRA HIRSC**[...]

In his book *The Road Trip That Changed the World*, Mark Sayers invites us to take a seat next to him as he guides us through the landscape of church, culture, consumerism, Christianity, religion, and faith. In the end, we can arrive at a place we long for: Home. A home not found in a creation of materials or in a geographical space but wonderfully discovered in a relationship with Jesus.

  —**DAVE GIBBONS**, Founder of Xealot.org and Newsong Church,
   and author of *XEALOTS*

As a keen student of culture, Mark Sayers unpacks how the primary narrative we inhabit will either lead us on the road, trying to capture as many "whoosh" experiences as we can, or enable us to take the road less traveled. If the church is going to answer her sacred calling and not allow the culture of the road to squeeze the life out of her, this book is a must-read!

  —**JR WOODWARD**, Cofounder of the Ecclesia Network and Kairos Los Angeles;
   author of *Creating a Missional Culture*

Many writers can exegete the Bible, few can exegete our culture. Mark Sayers does both with illuminating clarity and perception. *The Road Trip That Changed the World* is masterful depiction of our media-saturated world and the subtleties of its influence. Through the unique intersection of faith and culture, Mark's observations are fresh, timely, buoyant, and full of hope.

  —**DARREN WHITEHEAD**, Author of *Rumors of God* (with Jon Tyson),
   Teaching Pastor, Willow Creek Community Church

This is a book I wish I had written but know I never could. In a mesmerizing blend of anecdote and literature, pop sensitivity and cultural analysis, earthiness and biblical reflection, Mark Sayers gracefully calls the "travelers" of the world and the church home—via the signpost of a cross. Brilliant!

  —**DR. JOHN DICKSON**, Author, Historian, and Director
   of the Centre for Public Christianity

Mark Sayers again proves himself to be a state-of-the-art connoisseur of the times in which we live. *The Road Trip That Changed the World* is a brilliant and gripping portrayal of what ails church and culture, combined with the redemptive wisdom of how to fix it. People stream into our Swiss L'Abri community from all over the world. They deeply struggle with a myriad of issues, including which direction to take in life. So many roads go nowhere. Sayers's book, by contrast, is an exceptionally valuable guide that can decisively help counter dead ends and lead us home. I highly recommend it. This is a vital read. Sayers at his best.

  —**DR. GREGORY J. LAUGHERY**, Author, *Spiritual Rhythms For Today*,
   and Director of L'Abri Fellowship, Switzerland.

If you desire to better understand the condition of a culture that has lost its sense of the transcendent then pick up *The Road Trip That Changed the World*. As a pastor in a secular global city, I find Mark's writings to be an invaluable resource for understanding the soul of my city and learning how to address its hopes, angsts, and aspirations with the gospel.

    —**JR VASSAR**, Lead Pastor of Apostles Church, NYC

Mark Sayers once again skewers the cultural narrative we have been given and, while it wriggles impotently, invites us instead to make our home in the Story of God. Rich with cultural, personal, and biblical insight, *The Road Trip That Changed the World* leads us down the dusty path countless feet have trodden that results in our becoming truly human. Highly recommended.

    —**SEAN GLADDING**, Author of *The Story of God, the Story of Us*

This book will at once make you very uncomfortable and inspire you to take a fresh look at the true influences of your life. Will "the road" or the One who calls us to serve those on it be the dominate influence in our lives? Will we be the Church?

    —**ELLIS BRUST,** Lead Pastor, Epiphany Anglican Church,
    Orange County, California

Mark Sayers is one of the best readers and analysts of culture that I have met and read. In his new book he takes us on a road trip through our Western culture and shows what it is that is shaping and what has shaped our culture. This is a must-read for all who want to find a way of discipleship and mission in a Western context.

    —**THOMAS WILLER**, Sociologist and Pastor of Regen Church, Copenhagen

The Road Trip That Changed the World exposes our modern obsession with novelty, entertainment, and self-actualization while sketching a compelling vision for a biblical alternative. Mark Sayers is a keen exegete of contemporary culture and a wise guide for true seekers. He's written an important book that will help readers name, and resist, the gods of this age.

    —**DREW DYCK**, Managing Editor of *Leadership Journal*
    and author of *Generation Ex-Christian*

Mark Sayers's gifts as a cultural critic, theologian, and storyteller are all on fine display in this remarkable and well-written analysis of Western culture. Through the prism of Jack Kerouac's novel *On The Road*, Sayers tells the story of our culture and then offers a better way—a way home—through his reflections on God's call of Abraham. This, and much more, make *The Road Trip That Changed the World* a gripping and profound work.

    —**DOUGLAS GROOTHUIS,** Professor of Philosophy, Denver Seminary, and author
    of *Christian Apologetics: A Comprehensive Case for Biblical Faith*

Mark Sayers is a thoughtful, insightful, and observant leader who will push your thinking. At times he will make you mad. At times he will make you shout with affirmation. But you will not come away from this book unchanged. I'm thankful for his voice into the wider church world.

    —**GENE APPEL**, Senior Pastor, Eastside Christian Church, Anaheim, California

We often talk about what "culture" is doing to "them." We rarely think deeply about what "culture" is doing to "us." Sayers reveals what our cultural addiction to infinite choice has done to our stability as individuals—both inside and outside the church. *The Road Trip That Changed the World* is a terrific work of cultural hermeneutics, and we need to take Mark's challenges very seriously.

    —**JOHN STONESTREET**, Speaker and Author for Breakpoint and Summit Ministries

THE ROAD TRIP
THAT CHANGED THE WORLD

THE UNLIKELY THEORY THAT
WILL CHANGE HOW YOU VIEW
CULTURE, THE CHURCH, AND
MOST IMPORTANTLY, YOURSELF

Mark Sayers

MOODY PUBLISHERS
CHICAGO

All scripture quotations, unless otherwise indicated, are taken from
the *Holy Bible, New International Version*®, NIV®. Copyright © 1973, 1978, 1984,
2011 by Biblica, Inc.™ Used by permission of Zondervan. All rights reserved world-
wide. www.zondervan.com. The "NIV" and "New International Version" are trade-
marks registered in the United States Patent and Trademark Office by Biblica, Inc.™

All websites listed herein are accurate at the time of publication,
but may change in the future or cease to exist. The listing of website
references and resources does not imply publisher endorsement of
the site's entire contents. Groups, corporations, and organizations are
listed for informational purposes, and listing does not imply publisher
endorsement of their activities.

Edited by Elizabeth Cody Newenhuyse
Interior design: Smartt Guys design
Cover design: Matt Deutscher, Oak and Ink

Library of Congress Cataloging-in-Publication Data
Sayers, Mark.
    The road trip that changed the world : the unlikely theory that will
change how you view culture, the church, and most importantly, yourself /
Mark Sayers.
       p. cm.
    Includes bibliographical references (p.   ).
    ISBN 978-0-8024-0931-7
    1. Christian life. 2. Christianity and culture. 3. Kerouac, Jack,
1922-1969—Criticism and interpretation. I. Title.
    BV4501.3.S2855 2012
    248.4—dc23
                                          2012003882

We hope you enjoy this book from Moody Publishers. Our goal is
to provide high-quality, thought-provoking books and products that connect
truth to your real needs and challenges. For more information on other books
and products written and produced from a biblical perspective,
go to www.moodypublishers.com or write to:

Moody Publishers
820 N. LaSalle Boulevard
Chicago, IL 60610

1 3 5 7 9 10 8 6 4 2

Printed in the United States of America

My love,
Excited to read this with you as we figure out our journey. There is so much for us to learn and unlearn and I'm thrilled that you are my partner in all of this. Let's dive in and have our world view changed yet again, shall we? :)

For my children: Grace, Hudson, and Billy

I love you and I love your heart,

Your adventure buddy,

Natalie

CONTENTS

The expanse of the highway rolls out before us offering the tantalizing possibility of freedom. The horizon invites us forward, its hidden promise urging us to accelerate into the future. Behind us our pasts and our pains mingle with the exhaust fumes and evaporate into the cooling night air. Ahead the taillights bleed into streaks of color. The telephone poles beat out a rhythm, and almost unconsciously our foot presses the accelerator closer to the floor.

As the speedometer inches higher the act of driving becomes visceral. Flesh and metal become one, the automobile an extension of ourselves, a speeding incarnation of our wills. Yet the thrill of speed and the romance of the open road before us cannot mask the truth that we are lost. We have no map; out here there is no cell phone coverage. The robotic, manufactured voice of the GPS fell silent long ago. All we know is that we don't want to be where we have come from, and we are not sure where we are going. So for now our home is the road.

* *

PART 1

ONE:
A TALE OF TWO ROADS

"Whither goest thou, America, in thy shiny car in the night?"
Carlo Marx in Jack Kerouac's *On the Road*

"Nobody move, everything will be OK."
Mohamed Atta

In their chinos, casual shirts, and T-shirts they even dressed like writer Jack Kerouac. And although they had probably never read his classic novel *On the Road,* they were imitating Kerouac's vision of life to a T, living in cheap motels, sleeping in rental cars, criss-crossing their way around America. Through their lifelong exposure to popular culture, they had imbibed the life script for twentysome-things that Kerouac had sketched out almost half a century earlier. They were in a limbo, existing on the American road.

A delayed adolescence marked the culture of their group. Theirs was an all-male world. Yet long-distance phone calls to girlfriends, parents, and neglected wives betrayed an internal conflict between a desire for domestic bliss and an unfettered pursuit of pleasure. Kerouac was drawn to the seedy side of American life, so were the boys, they also liked strip clubs and dive bars. In Florida they rented scooters, speeding up and down the beaches.

They also seemed to have a weakness for glazed donuts, visiting convenience stores to sugar-load several times a day.[1]

The group had traveled en masse to Las Vegas, where they stayed in "cheap hotels on a dreary stretch of the Strip frequented by dope dealers and $10 street hookers."[2] The sons of the wealthy were slumming it, and just like Kerouac would regularly be seen staggering drunk or stoned on hash. Other nights they would go up-market and splash the cash on lap dances and expensive champagnes.[3]

Their public displays of arrogance and excess ensured that women would be seen on their arms. When they were not in the clubs they were buying porn,[4] and paying for sex with prostitutes in their hotel rooms. Their behavior could have been the script for an MTV reality show or a B-grade spring break movie, a lifestyle unintentionally championed by Kerouac on the fringes of American life. A vision of life that would in our time be pushed to the center, becoming typical and expected.

Yet these men were far from typical. Their wild living was a precursor of something more sinister.

A COCKTAIL OF FAITH AND VICE

Jack Kerouac lived out a contradiction. Raised a conservative Catholic, he maintained a love for and relationship with Christ for his whole life. Even in his most debauched moments his Bible was never far from his side. At times he was prudish and conservative, at other times a libertine. The young men in the group were the same. Like Kerouac, their actions were also contradictory. One moment they were deeply religious, praying late into the night and poring over scriptures; the next moment their behavior was marked by an unrestrained indulgence in vice.

Both Kerouac and the young men were drawn to and yet felt like outsiders in American life. Both wished for a death that would see them leave this world and find union with God in paradise.

Kerouac's journey to find God would take the form of a modern pilgrimage, with off-ramps and excursions into drug-fueled hallucinations, and dalliances with Buddhism and Taoism. Eventually, his body broken and addicted, he would return to his childhood devotion, spending his last days focused on Christ and the Cross. The young men would take a very different road in their quest to please God.

GO, GO, GO!

Popular culture chooses to ignore the middle-aged, worn-out Kerouac, hip to the futility of the American dream and the reality of sin, spending his last days meditating on the Cross. Instead it prefers the romantic vision of the handsome, twentysomething seminal hipster of *On the Road*. Speeding across America in a beat-up car that flew like a rocket, high as a kite, pretty girls in the back, jazz pouring out of the radio. His wild buddy and partner in crime Neal Cassady next to him like a fan at a jazz club, screaming GO, GO, GO out the window into the impossibly starry expanse of the Midwestern sky.

THAT MORNING THE NEW YORK STREETS THAT KEROUAC HAD WALKED HALF A CENTURY EARLIER WITH HIS FRIENDS WERE SHOWERED IN THE CONCRETE DUST OF THE WORLD TRADE CENTER.

The young men would also be remembered for posterity, flying across America at high speed, not on an impossibly starry night, but on an impossibly blue-skied morning. Their shouts would not be jazz-inspired slang. Instead they would be guttural and Arabic, screamed last words of "*Allahu Akbar.*" That morning the New York streets that Kerouac had walked half a century earlier with his friends were showered in the concrete dust of the World Trade Center and the vaporized remains of Mohamed Atta and his friends, known to history as the 9/11 hijackers.

CONTRADICTIONS

To us the behavior of the 9/11 hijackers seems strange. These were terrorists. A group of militants committed to a radical interpretation of Islam. A cell of men who were ready to offer their lives to defeat an enemy that they saw as morally degenerate. Men whose idea of modesty ensured that they covered with towels frames on their walls that contained some old photos of women bathing in 1920s swimming costumes, yet who happily would visit strip clubs.

The contradictory behavior of the 9/11 hijackers has confused analysts. Yet when examined in the light of our culture's true nature, the behavior of the group is not that shocking. Humans are contradictory creatures: we like to be logical, but our actions, wants, and desires are a far more confusing and inconsistent affair.

The majority of the 9/11 attackers were from upper- or middle-class families. Many, like the group's leader Mohamed Atta, had spent time living and studying in the West and felt strongly the tension between the worldview of the West and their adherence and loyalty to their own worldview and religion. The propaganda of Al Qaeda would point to various rationales for its war on the West, such as Western foreign policy, the existence of the state of Israel, and so on, but the hijackers' last moments giving into temptation illustrates a deeper and more implicit motive. They viewed the West as a culture that had thrown off any kind of restraint. Their last gasp giving into the fleshly temptations of the West was an admission to its seductive power and a confirmation of its need to be destroyed. Christianity and Judaism were seen as impotent and inferior because they had failed to rein in this new secular self with all of its base desires and personal freedoms.

The hijackers unintentionally found themselves caught between two visions of being human that would come to dominate the consciousness of the world at the beginning of the twenty-first century. To understand this tension more fully and appreciate its pull, not just on the lives of the 9/11 hijackers but on our own, we must now travel back to the period just after World War II. Back to the same Manhattan streets that Mohamed Atta would cover in ash, streets that in 1948 two men walked, reveling in and wrestling with the new culture that was emerging in the West. Two men who would create two philosophical roads.

TAKING A TEMPTING BITE OUT OF THE BIG APPLE

During a two-year period between 1947 and 1948, two young men lived in New York City. Both men were aspiring writers, both had reached a crossroads in their personal lives, both felt that Western culture had descended into a spiritual and existential crisis. Both men would end up writing bestselling books about this experience, works that would electrify generations to come, mold lifestyles, and offer visions of being human that would help shape the twenty-first century. Both in their own way would leave their marks not only on New York but on global culture. Both men would die early, in a manner that would appear as a kind of martyrdom to their followers. Their ideas would live on long after their deaths.

WHO WAS JACK KEROUAC?

Journalist Tom Brokaw would label Jack Kerouac's peers the "greatest generation," lauding their selflessness, work ethic, and commitment. This was the generation who understood material deprivation during the Great Depression, confronted the forces of fascism during World War II, and during the forties and fifties built America into the dominant global superpower.

Born in 1922, Kerouac was part of Brokaw's greatest generation, but his influence would shape the generation following his own. In a period of conformity and conservatism Kerouac would bounce around New York City in a ball of drug-fueled, jazz-inspired, sexual energy. Though unusual and deviant at the time, his lifestyle was far more like the typical young adults' of the twenty-first century—a lifestyle defined by a thirst for experience and travel, recreational drug use, a fear of and yet a desire for community and commitment. A promiscuous approach to sexuality, a desire to make it, a contradictory approach to faith, and few qualms about returning home to Mom when the money ran out.

For Kerouac, New York City was simply a starting point on a manic journey that would last for four years and that would crisscross the United States multiple times. This journey, part spiritual quest, part hedonistic romp, would inspire every road movie. Every buddy flick, every spring break bender, and every twentysomething, backpacking search to discover one's self that would follow over the coming decades owes something to Kerouac and his vision. Without Kerouac there could be no *Easy Rider*, no *Eat, Pray, Love*, no *Blue Like Jazz*. The details of this odyssey would be transformed into Kerouac's famous book *On the Road*, which is part confessional, part travelogue, and part novel.

WITHOUT KEROUAC THERE COULD BE NO EASY RIDER, NO EAT, PRAY, LOVE, NO BLUE LIKE JAZZ.

The book would be loosely autobiographical. *On the Road* tells the story of Kerouac and his friend Neal Cassady's numerous romps across the continental United States between 1947 and 1951. Since the book includes frank descriptions of the drug-fueled sexual misadventures of Kerouac's friends, his publishers worried about possible lawsuits. So they persuaded him to change the names to pseudonyms. Kerouac reinvented himself as Sal Paradise, and Neal became the legendary Dean Moriarty.

CATHOLIC, FRENCH-CANADIAN, AND CALVINIST

Kerouac was christened Jean Louis Lebris de Kerouac to French Canadian parents in Lowell, Massachusetts. Growing up in a French-speaking household, he did not speak English until he was six. The defining moment of his life was the tragic death of his brother Gerard from rheumatic fever at age nine. A survivor's sense of guilt haunted Kerouac for the rest of his life. His mother and father both loved God and the bottle — influences that would mark Kerouac's life and shape his grief. The French-speaking Catholics of Massachusetts followed the teachings of Cornelius Jansen, whose Catholicism was deeply influenced by the theology of John Calvin. This unique blend of Catholicism and Calvinism shaped Kerouac's faith, infusing it with a deep understanding of sin, the Cross, and the place of suffering in the Christian life.

> IF AMERICA WAS SETTLING DOWN BEHIND WHITE PICKET FENCES, THEY WANTED A LIFE ON THE ROAD.

A gifted football player, Kerouac earned a scholarship to Columbia University in Manhattan. Despite his athletic prowess and good looks, Kerouac found a home amongst a strange grouping of bohemian University buddies. The embryonic group consisted of poet Allen Ginsberg, writer William S. Burroughs, editor Lucien Carr, and various other misfits, bohemians, and artists. The group was united in their belief that American culture had gone awry. Their reading of Oswald Spengler's *Decline of the West* convinced them that they were living at the end of Western culture.

The group looked at a postwar society awash in materialism, secularism, and shallowness, and came to the belief that if rationalism and science had led society to its current crisis, then romanticism, spirituality, and experience would re-humanize America. The group found what they perceived as the strict and conservative moral confines of the forties stifling. They began to plot, plan, and live out a new way of being human, a response to the great crisis they saw all around them. If America was settling down behind white picket fences, they wanted a life on the road.

HOW A GROUP OF JAZZ FANS
SHAPED THE CONTEMPORARY SELF

The proximity of Columbia University to Harlem gave the group an appreciation of jazz and a somewhat naive and patronizing desire to imitate what they saw as the unfettered and authentic lives of African-Americans. This group of renegade bookworms also idolized other groups that they saw living on the edge of American culture, such as prostitutes, homosexuals, and petty criminals. Idolization would turn into imitation and eventually immersion as the group pushed the boundaries of acceptable social behavior, grounding themselves in the world of hustlers who hung around Times Square.

Unbeknownst to the group, their seminal experiments with sexuality, Eastern religions, drugs, and restless travel would be launched from the margins into the cultural mainstream over the coming decades. Kerouac labeled his friends the "Beat Generation"; later the media would dub them "beatniks," after the Sputnik satellite. The Beats would foreshadow the counterculture and the hippie movement of the sixties, which would in turn influence the mainstream in the seventies, and eventually come to define the contemporary consumer, popular culture, and personal questing in the West.

TWO:

HOW WORSHIP BECAME ENTERTAINMENT

Not disciples but spectators . . .

During the same eighteen-month period in which Kerouac and his friends were instigating their new mode of living on the edge of American culture, a young, well-dressed man arrived in the Big Apple. Like Kerouac, he was an unsuccessful novelist; he had a group of friends who read voraciously and hung out in cafes. Like Kerouac he sensed a spiritual danger in the postwar economic boom. He also was in the midst of a personal crisis. Unlike Kerouac's existential crisis over the death of his brother, this young man's crisis was ideological in nature. Like Kerouac he had grown up in a religious home. Sayyid Qutb, however, had been moving toward a more radical understanding of Islam in his homeland of Egypt. Yet at the same time he was drawn to modernization, and the West. His residency in the United States would spiritually, ideologically, and emotionally push him to his limits.

AL QAEDA AND THE ALL-AMERICAN GIRL

While Kerouac would throw himself guiltily into the hedonism of emerging postwar America, Qutb would recoil from it. Qutb tells the story of being woken on his ship over to America by a drunk woman who offered him sex. The encounter deeply shocked Qutb and shaped his interaction with and analysis of the United States. To Kerouac America was a seductress, inviting with her open expanses; spilling out westward she offered a new future of countless possibilities. To Qutb, America was a temptress sent by the devil to ensnare, entrap, and enslave. She was a danger, not just for the young, isolated, and homesick Muslim man but the entire Islamic world.

Sayyid, like Kerouac, could not help but notice the pulsating sexual energy of postwar America. The war had begun to change the social and sexual landscape. The conflict had taken young men away from women and a rediscovery of each other was occurring. Historian Robert S. Ellwood notes that the returning veterans brought back with them from the battlefields "newly uninhibited views on smoking, drinking, and sex."[1] The mobilization of women into the workforce during the war had given women a taste of equality, creating a new sense of boldness. This boldness was seductive to Kerouac who reveled in it with abandon. Qutb also noted this new spirit amongst mid-century American young women; however, to him it was repulsive, a sign of moral decay. In an essay on his time in America, Qutb wrote:

> The American girl is well acquainted with her body's seductive capacity. She knows it lies in the face, and in expressive eyes, and thirsty lips . . . she shows all this and does not hide it.[2]

The new American girl spoken of by Qutb could be readily found in the jazz clubs that Kerouac was drawn to. For Kerouac, jazz, particularly the sub-genre known as Bop, was transcendent, a kind of post-rational spiritual experience; an art form symbolic of a new future, and a new mode of humanity. Again Kerouac's view was in sharp contrast to Qutb, who offered this evaluation of American jazz music:

> The American is primitive. . . . Jazz music is his music of choice. It is this music that the savage bushmen created to satisfy their primitive desires, and their desire for noise on the one hand, and the abundance of animal noises on the other. The American's enjoyment of jazz does not fully begin until he couples it with singing like crude screaming. And the louder the noise of the voices and instruments, until it rings in the ears to an unbearable degree, the greater the appreciation of the listeners.[3]

Evaluating the responses of the two men, it would be easy at this point for us to write off Kerouac as a pioneer of the hedonism that has come to define youth and young adult culture in the West. It would also be equally tempting to dismiss Qutb's analysis as at best prudish and at worst bigoted. Both men, however, despite their limitations, noted cracks in Western culture that would turn into full-blown chasms. Both men through their writings would suggest new responses, new ways of being human that would radically change the spiritual landscape of the West.

KEROUAC'S ANSWER: THE RUCKSACK REVOLUTION

Kerouac would call for a "rucksack revolution," a generational move away from home on to the road, a new kind of lifestyle for young people that would be built upon experience, pleasure, spiritual exploration, mobility, and self-discovery. Kerouac would write that he saw "a vision of a great rucksack revolution thousands or even millions of young Americans wandering around with rucksacks."[4] For Kerouac this revolution would be a way of resisting what he saw as the secularizing and stupefying effects of mass consumer culture. His hope was founded in a sense that a new generation with a new vision for humanity, was:

> refusing to subscribe to the general demand that they con-
> sume production and therefore have to work for the privilege of
> consuming, all that . . . they didn't really want anyway such as
> refrigerators, TV sets, cars, at least new fancy cars, certain hair
> oils and deodorants and general junk you finally always see a
> week later in the garbage anyway, all of them imprisoned in a
> system of work, produce, consume, work, produce, consume.[5]

More than any other of his works, it was the publication of *On the Road* that would cast Kerouac into the media spotlight. The book would operate as a template for the new young-adult culture that would emerge over the coming decades. Slowly and surely his influence would be felt across New York, as his soft bohemianism would become the new mode of living communicated out from the city across the world through the channels of media, fashion, entertainment, and the industry of cool. Kerouac's unintended New York legacy can be found not just in the bars and cafes of Greenwich Village which he haunted, but also in the offices of MTV, *Playboy,* and Levis. In contrast Qutb would mostly be forgotten in New York. That is, until several decades later, when the young men of Al Qaeda, inspired by his writings, would fly commercial jets into both the World Trade Center towers and the consciousness of the West.

"ALL OF THEM IMPRISONED IN A SYSTEM OF WORK, PRODUCE, CONSUME, WORK, PRODUCE, CONSUME."

THE ROAD TO JIHAD

Qutb would also write a book based on his conclusions from his time in America, titled *Milestones*. Ironically Qutb would include a section in his work entitled "This Is the Road." Qutb's road was not Kerouac's open road of exploration; rather it was the road toward Shari'a law. Qutb not only would emerge from his time in America with a more radicalized view of Islam, he would become through his writings the spiritual guide of Al Qaeda's brand of Islam, personally inspiring the movement's two founders Ayman al-Zawahiri and Osama bin Laden. Virtually unknown in the West, Qutb would go on to be what the *Guardian* newspaper would label as "the most famous personality of the Muslim world in the second half of the 20th century."[6]

Living in the days after World War II, Qutb and Kerouac both sensed that a dramatic shift had occurred in Western culture. Both developed their own responses. Our journey in this book will follow Kerouac along his road—he will act as our guide to the culture that he helped create. Yet before we leave him behind, Qutb has some observations that will be foundational in our explorations of the way that our culture has shaped our lives and expressions of faith.

HOW CHURCH SWAPPED DEVOTION FOR ENTERTAINMENT

Like so many isolated foreign students in a new land, Qutb found himself attending churches in a search for support and friendship. He was shocked at what he found. For Qutb, Christianity would have not been a strange distant religion; as an Egyptian he would have grown up regularly rubbing shoulders with the significant Egyptian Coptic Christian minority. To Qutb's surprise the American church was not based around devotion and worship, but rather entertainment:

> If the church is a place for worship in the entire Christian world, in America it is for everything but worship. You will find it difficult to differentiate between it and any other place. They

go to church for carousal and enjoyment, or, as they call it in their language "fun." Most who go there do so out of necessary social tradition, and it is a place for meeting and friendship, and to spend a nice time. This is not only the feeling of the people, but it is also the feeling of the men of the church and its ministers.[7]

Qutb notes that the primary engine driving the postwar American soul was a desire for pleasure and the stimulation of the senses. Entertainment was the means of delivering the emerging postwar citizen these things. Facing the growth of secularism and a shrinking cultural influence, the Church felt this need to deliver its gospel message in a way that would attract the rising postwar youth culture. The American Church had begun to realize that in a culture in which radio, the cinema, jazz, and the nightclub dominated the minds of the young, it had to compete in the entertainment stakes. Qutb continues:

"Every minister attempts to attract to his church as many people as possible, especially since there is a tremendous competition between churches of different denominations. And for this reason, each church races to advertise itself with lit, colored signs on the doors and walls to attract attention, and by presenting delightful programs to attract the people much in the same way as merchants or showmen or actors . . .There is nothing strange in this, for the minister does not feel that his job is any different from that of a theater manager, or that of a merchant. Success comes first and before everything, and the means are not important, and this success will reflect on him with fine results . . . It is his first measure of the way he feels and evaluates.[8]

"THE MINISTER DOES NOT FEEL THAT HIS JOB IS ANY DIFFERENT FROM THAT OF A THEATER MANAGER."

The Egyptian had noted one of the most important yet rarely named shifts in the religion of the West, a shift from devotion to entertainment, from discipleship to self-actualization.[9] Qutb's words anticipate the shape that the Church in the West would take in the coming decades. His observations could not be more apt in our current day, in which ministers wilt under the pressure of constantly shaping and shifting their churches to suit the wants and desires of their congregations for novelty and entertainment. From our vantage point in history on this side of the events of 9/11, one cannot but speculate what might have happened if the isolated Egyptian, alone, far from home, open enough to visit a church, had discovered a vibrant American Church that vigorously engaged with the culture, that offered a critique of and response to the emerging culture of entertainment. Despite being misguided about so many other things, Qutb reveals to us a vital change in the nature of the Church in the West that so many have missed.

LISTENING AND OBSERVING FROM MY CHAIR IN THE FRONT ROW I COULD SEE THAT THE COLLECTIVE HAPPINESS OF THE TEAM PRODUCING THE EVENT WAS DEPENDENT ON THE NUMBER OF ATTENDEES WHO TURNED UP.

HOW CHURCH CHANGED

I pulled up, parked the car, and headed for the door of the church. Behind the stage whole teams sweated and slaved to ensure a high-quality event. The band, visibly under pressure, rehearsed, their conversation strained. For a few moments I thought an argument would break out. The pastor was stressed, and moved about the auditorium checking that his leaders were discharging their various duties. The seemingly giant media team buzzed around in a funk of sweaty annoyance.

Listening and observing from my chair in the front row I could see that the collective happiness of the team producing the event was dependent on the number of attendees who turned up. A giant clock appeared on the screen and began to count down to start time. This device did not seem to affect the punctuality of the attenders who dribbled in over the next fifteen minutes. The next forty minutes was a combination of phenomenal music, amazing media, and a lighting and sound system that most secular venues would have been jealous of. The video announcements offered attenders a virtual cornucopia of options, programs, and activities.

I turned around and looked out into the audience as the last song before my talk was being played. The front row comprised the church leaders, all of whom were engaged enthusiastically in the worship, but as I looked deeper into the congregation I noticed that the rest of the congregation stood, at worst not singing, at best halfheartedly mouthing the words. Almost every expression was blank as the colored lights flashed across their faces. Arms were crossed, gum was being chewed: the audience was the epitome of passivity.

They were not participants but consumers of a spectacle, not disciples but spectators. In that moment images of Jesus poured into my mind. Jesus walking through the silence of the desert, Jesus walking the dusty paths of Israel, announcing the kingdom of God. Shaping, disciplining, and teaching His disciples. Jesus on the cross giving up His life for the world, Jesus rising on the third day to inaugurate a new world. Instantly I was back in the auditorium, now myself staring at the show on stage like a deer caught in headlights. I shook my head at the disparity of the images in my mind and what I had just experienced.

In the past I would have blamed the church. I would have with coldness deconstructed the service. Looked down at my nose at the methodology. The problem is that I now have seen the same look of detachment in Reformed gospel preaching churches, hip emerging churches, and polished Pentecostal services. I have seen the same bored eyes in liturgical-heavy high churches and casual, organic house churches. The people who were running this church were great people, they were passionate about Jesus and sharing His mission with the world. They were dedicated to creating disciples. Yet something had fundamentally shifted. The balance of power had moved, but everyone was too busy trying to get the "undecideds" in the door to notice what had happened. My friends at the church faced an almost impossible task: satiating the hungry beast that is the twenty-first-century citizen of the West.

In the last months of World War II, Christian thinker Elton Trueblood worried about what culture would spring up in the postwar environment. Like Kerouac and Qutb, Trueblood sensed a profound social and spiritual threat facing the West. Trueblood would forcefully pour out his ideas in a small yet powerful book, *The Predicament of Modern Man*. Trueblood feared that as the West secularized, it would attempt to retain the morals of Christianity, yet detach itself from faith. Trueblood worried that in this context a new kind of believer would emerge, one who did not need Church or a faith community, but instead who followed a self-constructed form of religion.

In the postwar culture Trueblood feared not the death of the Church, but rather that the Church was being overrun by a new kind of member. One who was devoid of devotion, who held to faith lightly. Trueblood would write, "Unless this situation is altered, there is little hope for our civilization."[10] Trueblood passionately called for a new kind of Church to emerge, one which was filled with the devoted, the passionate, and the committed. For Trueblood this was not only the only hope for the Church, but the only hope for the West. I shudder to think what Trueblood would think of the Christian culture in the West today—a culture that has chosen to replace the ideal of religious devotion with the idol of individual freedom and aversion to commitment.

YOU MEAN YOU MEET HERE EVERY WEEK?

In my early twenties I had bought the mantra that in order to win over the reluctant masses of the developed West, all the Church had to do was to make itself look nothing like Church. So each Sunday night we would engage in a creative worship orgy, a service carefully engineered to look nothing like the typical Sunday service. On any given night anything could happen. There could be projections on the roof, experimental electronic music, obscure readings, interactive spaces, video mashups, or installation art. I was fueled by the belief that if we reached some mystical creative level of worship that somehow my city's hip young seekers would fill our space. Really the only people who would stumble into our cavernous space were mostly confused homeless people, who became even more confused as they tried to work out what on earth we were doing. Try explaining missional church in a postmodern age to a guy who just wants money for a train ride home.

I WAS FUELED BY THE BELIEF THAT IF WE REACHED SOME MYSTICAL CREATIVE LEVEL OF WORSHIP THAT SOMEHOW MY CITY'S HIP YOUNG SEEKERS WOULD FILL OUR SPACE.

We had been running a series featuring classic movies, using them as springboards into discussions about biblical themes. We had gone to extraordinary lengths to plan an entire service around *Charlie and the Chocolate Factory*. We had transformed the worship space into something resembling Willy Wonka's chocolate factory, there were clips from the film, candy hanging from the roof. It was simply the most creative service that I have ever experienced in a church. My wife had brought along a friend. She was exactly the kind of person we were trying to entice into church. Intelligent, hip and raised in the secular soup. She sat politely through the service, attentively listening. After the service my wife and I were anxious to know what she thought of the whole thing. She told us that she had a question. I prepared myself, I was poised ready to answer any question ranging from the exclusivity of Christ in a pluralistic society to objections against Christianity based on the Crusades. She looked at me and asked, "So will you guys be here next week?" Surprised at the seemingly banal question I replied in the affirmative. "What about the week after?" she asked. Again I replied yes. "So how long will you guys go to church on a Sunday?" she asked with an increasingly puzzled look on her face. "Indefinitely," I replied. "But what if you have something on?" she again asked. "We make this a priority. We are committed to coming here," I said. "That is so weird," she said, frowning and shaking her head in confusion. The initial barrier to faith for her was not a doctrinal issue, nor one of the hot topics of the day, neither was it about the shape of Church. Rather it was simply that the individual would reduce their options by promising to turn up to a place in time and space for the rest of their lives. For someone who was immersed in the culture of the road, the rhythms and commitments of faith were almost incomprehensible.

FOR SOMEONE WHO WAS IMMERSED IN THE CULTURE OF THE ROAD, THE RHYTHMS AND COMMITMENTS OF FAITH WERE ALMOST INCOMPREHENSIBLE.

As I look out my office window I am confronted by the solidity of the Gothic-inspired church across the road. It is squat, heavy, and gray. It looks like it could survive an artillery barrage. A remnant of the Christianity of medieval Europe, it looks completely out of place here next to a 7-Eleven, surrounded by offices and apartments. Built to last centuries, it will outlive you and me. Its architectural vision emerged from a worldview that praised stability, a worldview that in the early sixth century ordered monks not to wander, but to stay in place. It was built in a time when the Christian imagination built itself around ideas like the "rock of ages" and words like *obedience, eternity, foundation,* and *devotion*.

Yet listen to how differently we describe faith today. Yes, we still adhere to Christianity but our language has changed, revealing how we have submitted to the worldview of the road. We use terms like journey, feeling, and experience. The word *awesome* is everywhere, not so much describing a transcendent idea of God, but a transcendent experience—which in the current language of faith can be used interchangeably between a worship service and an alpine skiing tour of New Zealand. Our language exposes a new way of holding to faith, one that is short-term, feelings-based, and fragile. Something has fundamentally changed.

HOW TODAY'S YOUNG ADULTS HAVE BECOME REFUGEES OF FAITH

Today our religious lives are defined by a kind of traveling, a search to find the right church, the right expression of faith that delivers the right lifestyle. To contemporary sensibilities it seems ludicrous, but in the past people attended Church through a sense of duty and responsibility. A decision to attend Church was not made with individuals' wants, desires, and needs in mind. Rather Church attendance was part of the fabric of spiritual discipline. Today people without an ounce of shame admit that they are "church shopping." Like good consumers we compare the various attributes of churches, looking for the Christian community that will best assist us in achieving our predetermined life goals.

Some will note that the culture of transience that we find both in the Church and in the wider culture is caused by an economy in which many change jobs and thus homes regularly. Yet its real engine lies deeper in the human soul. Philosophers Hubert Dreyfus and Sean Dorrance Kelly explain, "To say that we live in a secular age in the modern West is to say that even religious believers face existential questions about how to live a life."[11] Ours is a culture in which a constant searching for happiness is the ultimate goal, meaning that believers find themselves constantly reevaluating their faith, testing that faith's ability to deliver our culture's vision of the good life.

Due to the cultural waters in which we swim, a set of non-biblical expectations have attached themselves to our faiths, fueling our quest for a dizzyingly blissful vision of life this side of eternity. When disappointed in the quality of their lives, many people—particularly young adults across the Western world—blame not their overblown expectations but instead their faiths, abandoning in droves their engagement with Christianity.

ONE RELIGIOUS SOCIOLOGIST I HEARD INTERVIEWED NOTED THAT FOR MANY YOUNG ADULTS CHRISTIANITY IS NOW JUST A LIFE STAGE.

One religious sociologist I heard interviewed noted that for many young adults Christianity is now just a life stage, an experiment of adolescence. This reduces Christianity to just one of many offerings that the individual samples during their life in the quest for the good life. These heightened expectations of faith and radical individualism present an incredible challenge to faith. Sociologist Wade Clark Roof has observed that "the real story of American religious life in this half-century is the rise of a new sovereign self that defines and sets limits on the very meaning of the divine."[12] Rabbi Shmuley Boteach, commenting on the religiosity of contemporary culture, notes that in the West we now have "a generation whose principal desire is to feel [God] rather than worship Him."[13] In such a climate, faith becomes just one rest stop on the highway of life.

THREE:
FROM HOME TO THE ROAD

"All of man's misfortune comes from one thing, which is not knowing how to sit quietly in a room."
Blaise Pascal in *Pensées*

After fourteen hours in the air, my back is stiff and my mouth is filled with a horrible taste. We left Melbourne, Australia, as smiling human beings. Yet somewhere over the Pacific we have morphed into sleepless zombies, packed into a metal fuselage. The pilot's voice crackles over the public address system, telling us that we will soon be making our descent into Los Angeles. I have now been awake for almost thirty hours. Despite how terrible I feel I cannot switch off my mind. The cultural radar inside of me continues to pulse. Trying to orient myself, I peer out of the window as we float over the City of Angels. I spot the 101, the Hollywood Freeway.

The Hollywood Freeway was built in 1925, when the emerging industries of cinema and the motor car were creating a new sense of the modern. The individual, no longer tethered to a piece of dirt, could take off down the open road of self-discovery, with movie-inspired dreams of personal reinvention. My dog-eared copy of *The Penguin History of the USA* has on its cover the image of an open road, leading through an expansive desert, disappearing over the horizon. It is the iconic American symbol. As I look down at the freeway below me, snaking through the Hollywood Hills, linking with ten thousand other roads, each representing ten thousand possibilities, I think of America immense in its geography and its dreaming, and I think of Jack Kerouac.

In 1947 Jack Kerouac set off on a road trip that would reshape the mental landscape of almost everyone born in the West since that date. His cross-country jaunt would change how we viewed the world, processed our lives, and interacted with our faiths. It would alter the cultural code of the West, reorientating our collective psyches around the idea of the road.

Kerouac recorded his road trips in his classic book *On the Road*. Even if you have never read the book, you have been influenced by it.[1] It, almost more than any other work, laid the foundation for the culture of the road. It would ensure that Kerouac for decades would operate as a kind of template for the cool, brooding hipster—would be a sort of grandfather for punk, indie, and everything cool that has come since.

I first read *On the Road* years ago and found the book anticlimactic. The counterculture bible did nothing for me. The hedonistic, transient, and self-absorbed lifestyles of Kerouac's characters were on display all around me. They were groundbreaking and strange in the fifties but normal in our day.

Then I started reading *On the Road* for the second time and realized that what I was holding in my hand contained clues to how we had gotten to where we are. It was a vision of the lifestyles that were to come. It would be read by millions, but its approach to life would be imitated in one form or another by millions who had never read the book.

True, the release of the book did not change the culture single-handedly but tapped into the desire for change that was already bubbling under the surface. Kerouac's friend, the author William S. Burroughs, remarked, "The restlessness, the dissatisfaction were already there waiting when Kerouac pointed out the road."[2] Yet it was Kerouac's motif of the road that provided the spark that would ignite the fire of cultural change.

OUR CULTURAL IDEAL USED TO BE "HOME"

Before Kerouac changed the life script of the West, life was processed through the idea of home. Home was not just a building in which you lived. It was a place to which you were deeply connected. Home was a family and a community of people to whom you belonged. Home was a unified worldview. This worldview infused every part of your life: it informed your recreational life, your work life, your religious life, even your sex life. This sense of home was held together by traditions and a way of life to which the individual submitted.

Despite these traditions restricting options and personal freedoms, the ideal of home gave the individual a sense of purpose, belonging, and place. You did not need to discover who you were. Your sense of rootedness and your communal connections gave you a sense of self, an identity that was set and solid. Sure, not everyone experienced home in this way, but for the culture it was the ideal; a secure home and a loving community was what we hoped for. Journalist Thomas Friedman uses the symbol of the olive tree to describe this worldview of home:

> Olive trees are important. They represent everything that roots us, anchors us, identifies us and locates us in this world — whether it be belonging to a family, a community, a tribe, a nation, a religion or, most of all a place called home. Olive trees are what give us the warmth of family, the joy of individuality,

the intimacy of personal rituals, the depth of private relationships, as well as the confidence and security to reach out and
encounter others.[3]

Today we could not be in a more different space. No longer do
we view our lives through the ideal of home. Thanks to Jack Kerouac, our ideal is the road. We view life through the prism of the
journey. In contrast to the olive tree, Friedman uses the symbol of
the Lexus to illustrate the emerging contemporary worldview—
that is, a luxury vehicle for a new kind of individual who prefers
movement and individual autonomy to the stability and traditions
of the worldview of the olive tree.

HOW WE BEGAN TO SEE LIFE AS A JOURNEY

An award-winning commercial for Louis Vuitton exemplifies this
ideal. It features lush, cinematic shots of attractive individuals in
deserts, cities, and exotic locales. There is a deeply sensual tone
to the commercial. A suited man takes off his shoes and walks
barefoot on the Saharan sand. Another man stands before the
vista of an exquisite river, exhaling a cloud of visible breath in the
cool morning air. A young female traveler sleeping in the alcove of
a Tibetan village is awakened by the wind moving through her hair.
Pages rustle in a journal; a young man drinks in both his tea and
the sight of Shanghai at dawn. Across the screen come a series of
statements and questions:

> What is a journey?
> A journey is not a trip. It's not a vacation. It's a process.
> A discovery.
> It's a process of self-discovery.
> A journey brings us face to face with ourselves.
> Does the person create the journey, or does the journey create
> the person?

The journey is life itself.
Where will life take you?

It is easy to see why this commercial is award winning. It is beautifully shot, drenched with evocative images. Its romanticism resonates with us because it reveals one of the great values that our contemporary culture holds dear—that life is a journey. That true meaning and happiness are found on the road.

Another commercial, this one for a Ford sedan. The voiceover reads Robert Frost's poem "The Road Not Taken." An unsure young man with a backpack stands before two roads in a forest. He

"THE JOURNEY IS LIFE ITSELF. WHERE WILL LIFE TAKE YOU?"

chooses the unpaved road. Next a montage of shots. The young man traveling the world. Swimming in the sea. Laughing with an old man on a Greyhound bus. Making love with a beautiful young woman in the back of a van. Crying in a New York alleyway. Always walking or driving. Always on the road. His beard grows longer; his walk is now determined and devoid of its hesitation. In the final scene the young man is now older, driving a Ford sedan with his wife and children. He pulls over and picks up a young hitchhiker. Before driving off, he turns to the hitchhiker in the backseat and gives him a knowing and wise look. The unspoken message of the commercial is that he now can accept driving a family sedan with all its implications of home, responsibility, and maturity because he has lived the journey.

HOW OUR CULTURE OF CHOICE CREATED THE CULTURE OF THE ROAD

So why do we choose to view life as a journey? How did Kerouac's image of the road become so applicable to how we live and think? Well, modern life is a confusing business. The culture of home, in which everyone subscribed to one worldview, has disappeared. Now, every moment of our lives we are faced with countless decisions. The contemporary person is stuck in a constant quandary. Would I be happier in a smaller city? Should I eat more fruit? Am I overweight? Am I bisexual? Should I invest in the stock market? Android or iPhone? Do I need a vacation? Should I take up yoga? Am I stressed? Should I read more? What do I think of global warming? Sure, we have freedom of choice but we must navigate the immensity of the options before us.

Our confusion only increases when we understand the way that our culture segments our lives into compartments. We have our family lives, our work lives, our emotional lives, our sex lives, our spiritual lives, and our recreational lives. We have our finances and our fitness, our health and our political beliefs. Our culture tells us that to be happy we must find meaning and success in each of these areas. How do we do this? We are told that we must survey the immensity of choice in each segment and then make the right decision that will ensure happiness—a feat comparable to winning the lottery.

HOW DO WE CHART AND PLAN A LIFE OF MEANING AND HAPPINESS WHEN WE ARE CONFRONTED WITH SO MANY CHOICES?

There is a whole industry of magazines, books, websites, and TV shows dedicated to providing advice on how to achieve success and meaning in each life segment. This creates an anxiety in the individual. Contemporary life becomes a constant rolling of the dice to pull off the impossible. Our lives may be great, but if one area is not up to scratch, we feel that something is amiss. Thus we suffer from a permanent restlessness. How do we chart and plan a life of meaning and happiness when we are confronted with so many choices, so many contrasting worldviews and opinions, so many experiences, and so much information? This is where the motif of the road comes in.

The Russian thinker Mikhail Bakhtin, in his study of novels and films, observed that roads play a special role in plots. For the writer they are a useful way of creating meaning within complicated circumstances. For example, it would be hard to write a novel that captures the complexities and breadth of the giant country that is China. It is much easier to write a novel about two friends who decide to bicycle across China. Of course the people that they will meet on their journey and the events and places they experience will offer us a window of understanding into China. One which is palatable and does not leave us overwhelmed. In the same way we apply the motif of the road or the journey to our lives as a manageable way of understanding and processing our experiences in a world which has said good-bye to the culture of home.

HOW THE ROAD CREATED CHICKEN NUGGETS, PREMARITAL SEX, AND CHURCH SHOPPING

Initially Kerouac's vision of the road gave a new and controversial language and name to the way that postwar culture was reshaping the contemporary person. Over the coming decades Western culture would rearrange itself around the motif of the road. Watching hordes of young backpackers in Thailand, novelist Hari Kunzru observed that Kerouac's vision had moved from a radical countercultural statement to a "middle-class ritual."[4] The road is now woven into our culture's structures. We fail to notice this because we are so accustomed to the symbolism and narrative of the road, the most powerful cultural values are those which remain unnoticed. It is only when you stand at a distance, or leave your own culture, that you are able to recognize your own values for what they are.

The average person in the West carries around in their head a set of assumptions that are culturally imbibed. Assumptions such as the idea that spirituality is preferable to organized religion, that love is a feeling not a discipline, that if something is mundane it must be boring, that individual freedom trumps the collective, that travel broadens the mind, or that we can do what we like as long as it does not hurt anybody. All of these cultural ideas are elements that could fit into the worldview of the road. None of these values and ideas are taught in school; rather one picks them up the way we pick up a head cold. Philosopher James K. A. Smith reminds us that it is not just religions that disciple—our culture disciples us. According to Smith every structure of a culture carries a worldview and a form of teaching that "shape and constitute our identities by forming our most fundamental desires and our most basic attunement to the world. . . . They prime us to approach the world in a certain way, to value certain things, to aim for certain goals, to purse certain dreams . . . to be a certain kind of person."[5]

Of course, where there is a road, there are cars. The motor car, which gave Kerouac's characters their sense of personal freedom, was one of the key formational tools in shaping the contemporary person of the road.

HOW THE CAR CHANGED SEXUALITY IN THE WEST

Cultural critic Daniel Harris[6] points out that the motor car created youth culture, allowing young people the freedom to socialize outside of the family unit. Harris notes that the postwar popularity of the car created the space for the rise in premarital sex. Before the car, young people socialized cross-generationally in the family home. The rituals of courtship happened primarily within the home, and were done in community. Before the car, the social dynamics of home and community made premarital sex a logistical nightmare. Hotels and rooming houses would not allow unmarried couples to rent rooms. The arrival of the car created an accountability-free space in which teenagers for the first time in history could engage in intercourse outside of community. No longer was sex the apex of a communal process based on covenantal commitment, a reward for delayed gratification; intercourse could now happen in the back of a car on the first date.

HOW THE CAR CHANGED HOW WE EAT

The culture of the car would also lead to the invention of fast food, a portable, quickly delivered snack to be consumed either at a stop on the road, or in the car. The invention of the chicken nugget was the result of a fierce battle between rival fast food chains to find a form of chicken that could be eaten safely by a driver.[7] Food had traditionally been a communal affair, in which community and/ or family stopped to eat and socialize. Just as sex had been transformed by the possibility of individualism and instant gratification, food would be changed by the car. It is interesting that in France, which places a cultural value upon slow cooking and communal eating with local fresh produce and where children are taught as early as kindergarten to sit down for formal meals, obesity levels are minimal, whereas countries such as the United States which have embraced fast food are experiencing epidemics of obesity.

HOW THE CAR CHANGED HOW WE WORSHIP

The car also created the phenomenon that we know today as church shopping. Before the car, the parish and the neighborhood church dominated the religious landscape. However, the coming of the car meant that people could travel distances to find a church that suited their needs. Robert Schuller created a new kind of church when in the fifties, smack bang in the middle of the car culture that is Southern California, he started a church that was a combination of drive-in and worship service. Participants did not even have to leave their car: Schuller encouraged worshipers to "come as you are in the family car."[8] Schuller's church had been planted out of the Reformed tradition; however, when positive-thinking advocate Norman Vincent Peale would guest preach at his church, the drive-in service would be overflowing. Schuller responded and changed his preaching approach from a traditional gospel presentation to reflect Peale's Christian positive-thinking message. This move would radically alter the landscape of contemporary Christian culture in the coming decades.

Can we draw a line from the "car culture" of fifty years ago to the "always connected" culture of today? I think we can. In our day the Internet and social media offer what playwright Richard Foreman calls "the technology of the 'instantly available.'"[9] These technologies rewire our brains at a neurological level, making it difficult to concentrate, so that we graze over information and are permanently distractible.[10] Twenty years ago at an airport or at a train station people would talk to each other, or work their way through the long-form narrative of books. Now we sit in our electronic bubbles, headphones on, looking at our screens, scanning worlds of information, mental and emotional nomads. Thus our following of the culture of the road is not an intellectual decision; it is a habit of the heart which we have acquired through osmosis. We follow the culture of the road because it is everywhere, and as author Jon Tyson notes, "It's this 'everywhere' that shapes our lives."[11]

FOUR:
THE JOURNEY

"The open road is a beckoning, a strangeness, a place where a man can lose himself."
William Least Heat-Moon

Recently I watched an interview featuring a B-grade celebrity who had toiled away for fame through her rather mediocre music career. The interview followed her personal journey. The story began in stage one. Through a series of flashbacks we were shown the starlet in her younger days. She burst onto the scene with a pop song that garnered her initial fame. Then, however, a public backlash was followed by a time out of the media spotlight. Several relationship breakdowns and the supposedly horrifying arrival of the age of thirty had resulted in our starlet finding herself in stage two and facing obstacles.

Finally, according to the video montage, the starlet reached stage three. She gave up singing, instead focusing on hosting a reality TV show. Most importantly she had also met her "true love." She made sure everyone knew that this was all possible through the support of her close family and true friends who "believed in her through thick and thin." She then regurgitated out the jargon of the third stage. "I am now truly comfortable in my skin."

"I feel centered." "I am happy being me." And so on. The syco-
phantic interviewer then ended the interview by telling our beam-
ing starlet that she had "truly found happiness." The audience
exploded into a sustained ovation. Watching, I half-expected
the TV studio's roof to open and our starlet to ascend to the third
heaven, or perhaps morph into the Buddha. Instead, the only visible personal transformation in our starlet seemed to be the way
that her anatomy had been "augmented" since her early videos.

THE ROAD AS SECULAR PILGRIMAGE

The starlet's life was communicated to the audience as a form
of journey. The motif of journey is everywhere in our culture—in
film, in celebrity autobiographies, in advertisements for physical
fitness, in reality TV. Throughout history various religious traditions have used the imagery of pilgrimage or journey to describe
spiritual development. These journeys were focused on an eternal
destination, a spiritual transformation of the individual. Today,
however, the "pilgrimage" is all about the individual's own life
journey. In the past the individual gained a sense of solace knowing that despite life's disappointments and inevitable suffering,
meaning was still found in God's will for every individual. Sociologist Francesca Collins wonders, "Perhaps the 'journey' is a
secularized version of 'God's will.' It allows us to make sense of
the utterly unfathomable without resorting to God or some sort of
compensation in the afterlife."[1] By seeing life as a journey we can
enjoy the moral cost-free benefits of secular living, but then later
can Photoshop a layer of meaning over our lives by recounting our
experiences as part of our "life journey." The confusion, fragmentation, and randomness of living in a secular culture loses some of
its sting when we apply the "journey" tag to our messy lives.

    The notion expressed in Paulo Coelho's mega-selling novel

The Alchemist, in which the experience of the journey trumps the importance of the destination, permeates the contemporary mind-set. In his book *The Art of Travel*[2] philosopher Alain De Botton points out that the attraction of travel is not so much in the arriving at your destination, but rather the anticipation of destination. We are addicted to the thought of leaving, to tantalizing possibilities of where we could be going, rather than the concrete reality of actual arrival. We are addicted to being on the road, of having that next destination hovering over the horizon. Thus life, identity, and faith are now viewed as things in process, not yet fully formed. The security of knowing, of arriving, kills the buzz of the contemporary life journey.

The excellent research of Graham Cray, Sylvia Collins-Mayo, Bob Mayo, and Sara Savage illustrates for us the way that the symbol of the road has come to dominate the minds of young. The researchers discovered that traditional, transformative religious worldviews that gave a greater sense of meaning were not only missing from the lives of young people, but not missed:

> Lack of . . . religious sensibility did not appear to result in our young people feeling disenchanted, alienated or lost in a meaningless world. Instead, the data indicated that they found meaning and significance in the reality of everyday life, which the popular arts helped them to understand and imbibe. In this respect, we found a coherent narrative that underpins our young people's worldview. In essence, it states: "This world, and all life in it, is meaningful as it is." . . . There is no need to posit ultimate significance elsewhere beyond the immediate experience of everyday life. This means that . . . young people had no obvious need for what we call transformative spirituality.[3]

The team found that young people were not interested in

overarching stories that explained the world. Instead a smaller, coherent personal narrative that gave a sense of meaning to the individual was what the young people centered their lives around. Ideas like the eternal, heaven, or an afterlife were of little importance. Instead, real-time individual happiness and well-being was the ultimate goal. The journey has replaced the traditional religious means of processing and approaching life.

THE THREE STAGES OF THE ROAD

The young people surveyed perceived the life journey as a three-stage process. First, the individual aspires to be happy, to experience enjoyment and pleasure, and generally have fun. One did not need to look beyond the individual and the visible world to the spiritual for meaning; rather, purpose was found in experiencing all that the world had to offer. The wider implication of this belief is that if each individual pursued such a goal, everyone would be happy, and then society would be peaceful and unified.

Second, it was inevitable that the individual's journey toward happiness and well-being would be blocked. Blockages could be low self-esteem, negative body image, sexual abuse, lack of recognition, or the mundane. Through the unconditional acceptance and support of close friends and loved ones, through creativity, freedom and choice, and the collation of enriching experiences, the individual could move past the blockages. The obstacles of the second stage are the lessons of the road, the teachings of the journey of life. If the individual could overcome, or personally transcend, the obstacles to happiness, the last stage of the road was theirs. The final destination was the elusive quality of "personal growth." The person was now an "authentic individual"—one who had finally achieved happiness.

THE ROAD IS PERMANENT ADOLESCENCE

We like the idea of the road because it enables us to remain emotionally adolescent. Yet other cultures do not share our aversion to "settling down." Quite the opposite: After living with tribes of nomads, travel writer Bruce Chatwin discovered that one of the greatest tragedies of tribal life was to not be initiated into adulthood. Death was preferable. Uninitiated persons would remain on the outer edges of the community, never to be safely ensconced under the umbrellas of tribe or marriage. The uninitiated would never be seen to mature into men or women but were condemned to purposelessness. While the tribe traveled together, the uninitiated were left to journey alone—to eke out an existence on the edges of society, stuck in a permanent adolescence.

WE ARE LIVING IN THE MIDST OF A GRAND SOCIAL EXPERIMENT IN WHICH WE ARE ENCOURAGED TO LIVE IN A PERPETUAL ADOLESCENCE.

In our culture of the road, this situation is reversed. We are living in the midst of a grand social experiment in which we are encouraged to live in a perpetual adolescence, one that keeps us on the road, wandering individuals cut off from the tribe. Behind us is home, with the comforts of the familiar and a childlike sense of security. Yet we also want to leave home because of the restraints of parental authority. Ahead over the horizon is the potential of adulthood. The possibility of a mature life is appealing. Yet the responsibility and commitments of adulthood strike fear into the hearts of people raised in an adolescent culture. So instead of moving forward, or backward, many choose to stay on the road, accepting the permanent in-betweenness of the adolescent.

HOW OUR LOSTNESS CREATES THE ROAD

There are two migrations occurring in our world today. In the two-thirds world, countless people find themselves displaced

from home, fleeing war, famine, natural disaster, and environmental catastrophe in search of safety. For millions, home is now
the road, or the refugee camp. For these people movement is a
terrible necessity. These people find themselves with little control
over their lives; rather, they find themselves on the move. Looking
for a safe place to call home.

Then there is another group. This group is not only separated
from actual refugees and displaced people by geography but also
by wealth, opportunity, and privilege. In their book *Beyond Homelessness*,[4] Steven Bouma-Prediger and Brian J. Walsh contrast
the genuine refugee with the contemporary Westerner traveling
the world, fleeing relationships, changing jobs, and always on the
move—yet suffering a poverty of meaning, a loss of true home,
identity, and place. Bouma-Prediger and Walsh declare this root-
less lifestyle as a kind of psychic homelessness in which individuals lack a spiritual home.

BEING ON THE ROAD IS A MENTAL STATE

The contemporary self does not have to literally be on the move
to be on the road. Being on the road is primarily a state of mind,
one that constantly is dissatisfied, looking for the next best thing,
living in incompleteness, always engaged in a quest for a sense of
significance. This search for meaning becomes even more problematic in a culture which flees from objective truth, which fears
authority and the holding of belief too strongly. The contemporary
person finds themselves engaged in a quest for a truth they are
told that they cannot find. In which the act of questing itself is
given more importance than the completion of the quest. In such
an environment the worldview of the road is triumphant.

JESUS' VISION OF THE ROAD

The road has made us fickle. It has made our faiths weak. It has made us spoiled. To state it in its most brutal and blatant form, the road is ruining our lives and it is ruining our culture. It has left us lost and directionless, consumers not followers of God. When we open the pages of Scripture we find a different kind of person from the person of the road. A person of the way. The way of Christ. A pilgrim of a road that does not lead to the tantalizing potential of a future destination but instead to a wooden cross. A way that promises life eternal but that also demands total obedience, complete surrender, and death to self.

Jesus Himself taught that there are two roads. One road is wide and leads to destruction and death. The other road, although narrow, leads to life. This book is about those two roads. It is about what road you are going to follow. To find out how to take the narrow road, we must understand how we find ourselves constantly taking the wide road to destruction; we must explore how our culture sabotages our efforts to take the road to life.

FIVE:

THE SECULAR WORLD

"The voice inside your head has become a different voice.
It used to be 'you.' Now your voice is that of a perpetual nomad
drifting along a melting landscape, living day to day expecting
nothing and everything."
Douglas Coupland

In many ways the late nineteen-forties and fifties seemed like a rebirth for the Church in the West. In the United States as the suburbs grew and the economy boomed so did churches. Billy Graham gained rock star status and became the most traveled man in the world. Parachurch organizations and youth movements were in the ascendancy. Sayyid Qutb was shocked by the sheer number of churches to be found, commenting, "I once stayed in a town with no more than ten thousand inhabitants, yet within it I found over twenty churches!"[1] Qutb was puzzled that despite the many church buildings, the majority of Americans only seemed to attend the High Holidays of the Christian calendar.

HOW POSTWAR AMERICA TURNED INTO
A SPIRITUAL WASTELAND

Despite seemingly having an affection for Christianity and a respect for its traditions, Qutb found religion absent from the daily lives of Americans: "There is no one further than the American from appreciating the spirituality of religion and respect for its sacraments, and there is nothing farther from religion than the American's thinking and his feelings and manners."[2] What Qutb was discerning was a split in the Western soul. Secularism had not eradicated Christianity or the Church from the Western landscape, yet it had radically altered how faith was viewed. After two thousand years as the driving force in the Western heart, soul, and mind, the Church had been replaced by a new power, secularism. Reflecting on Qutb's analysis of Western spirituality, Pulitzer Prize–winning journalist Lawrence Wright comments:

IT WAS EASY TO BE MISLED BY THE PROLIFERATION OF CHURCHES, RELIGIOUS BOOKS, AND RELIGIOUS FESTIVALS.

> Qutb saw a spiritual wasteland, and yet belief in God was nearly unanimous in the United States at the time. It was easy to be misled by the proliferation of churches, religious books, and religious festivals, Qutb maintained; the fact remained that materialism was the real American god. . . . Many Americans were beginning to come to similar conclusions. The theme of alienation in American life was just beginning to cast a pall over the postwar party. In many respects, Qutb's analysis, though harsh, was only premature.[3]

Qutb was sensing the rumblings in American life that would soon turn into a full-scale earthquake in the coming decades. Beneath the veneer of Christian culture and adherence, the implicitly secular values of hedonism and materialism were growing in strength. Soon the traditions of faith that had remained for centuries would be torn asunder.

Kerouac also looked out across the expanse of postwar America and sensed a deadening in the American soul. The middle class was gaining an unparalleled level of material comfort, and yet it was also losing something. The spirituality of the country was being flattened. Mass production, consumerism, and secularism joined forces, throwing a blanket over the American soul, stifling its desires for transcendence and God. Instead, the new "gods" offered the trinkets of faux-immanence, be they Cadillacs, refrigerators, movie matinees, or skyscrapers. The secularism that Kerouac had intuitively observed emerging was not the dictionary definition of the term in which the Church's powers were kept separate from the public realm. Rather it was a much more insidious form of secularism, one which came in the night and stole the holy dreams and spiritual visions of the young.

Kerouac's writings were an attempt to awaken youth to a grand lie that was being peddled, that their lives and the world could be described only in the language of science and reason. Thus his goal as a writer, as observed by biographer John Leland, was "to show that . . . the world really is mysterious, supernatural, impervious to scientific or rational analysis."[4] Kerouac's call to the road was a call to return to a deeper understanding of life, in contrast to the shallowness of contemporary living. Secularism and the death of belief was a crisis.

Spurred on by this crisis, Kerouac "set out to do nothing less than to narrate 'soul' perceptions to an increasingly soulless American middle class hungry for revelations of life's everyday holy radiance."[5] Kerouac's call for a religious reawakening of the American soul was not received well by the intellectuals of his day—intellectuals whom he saw as atheistic, deluded, and detached from the real struggles of human life. Kerouac once joked that while the cultural elite despised his books, his true readers were the kids who stole his books from bookstores.

> KEROUAC "SET OUT TO DO NOTHING LESS THAN TO NARRATE 'SOUL' PERCEPTIONS TO AN INCREASINGLY SOULLESS AMERICAN MIDDLE CLASS HUNGRY FOR REVELATIONS OF LIFE'S EVERYDAY HOLY RADIANCE."

Kerouac had hit a cultural nerve amongst many growing up in a secular age, one made more terrible by the arrival of the atomic bomb. Kerouac's friend, the poet Allen Ginsberg, noted that the dropping of the atomic bomb upon the Japanese cities of Nagasaki and Hiroshima created what he described as a psychic disturbance amongst his friends, fueling their despair and subsequent drug use.[6] Kerouac labeled the spiritual crisis that had begun to infect his generation as the "atomic disease."[7]

THE ATOMIC BOMB AND THE ROAD

The culture of the road would be born out of the atomic age. The heat of the nuclear flashes over Nagasaki and Hiroshima marked the end of the West's hot war with the Axis forces, which soon subsided into the chill of the Cold War, a conflict that would shape culture in the West for the next fifty years. The Cold War created a strange in-between reality in which mass consumerism overtook the Western world, seemingly spurred on by the fact that an apocalyptic global nuclear war could break out at any moment. Symbolically, the nuclear attacks upon Japan created an open space into which new expressions of personhood could come of age. They also signaled a new age, in which science had given humanity a deathlike touch, a touch that had the power to undo the creation of the world.

MASS CULTURE GIVES BIRTH TO A MASS WANDERING

The mass culture of the postwar era craved stability after the horrors of the war. People sought to create this stability to offset the vision of the potential apocalypse that could be inflicted by a global nuclear conflict. So compared to what was to follow in the sixties, the forties and fifties are still remembered as a time of moral traditionalism. However, beneath this veneer of conformity and conservatism, the Western idea of person-hood continued to evolve.

The economy of the United States, namely the manufacturing sector, was turbocharged by the war. An unprecedented standard of living was spreading out across the country, a standard of living so high that visiting Soviet officials thought that they were being duped by a capitalist ruse. Mass production was giving birth to mass culture; mass culture would give birth to the road.

THE MEDIA OF THE DAY, FASCINATED WITH THE ARRIVAL OF THIS NEW KIND OF HUMAN, SPECULATED THAT NO DOUBT THIS QUIRKY BEHAVIOR EXHIBITED BY THE YOUNG WOULD DIE OUT AS "THEY GREW UP, GOT PROPER HAIRCUTS AND REAL JOBS."

During this period of growth, the postwar car culture reshaped America's landscape both physically and psychically. Bill Levitt's vision of suburbia reshaped understandings of community life, television transformed family lives, and a recharged Madison Avenue began to raise the public's expectations of what the "good life" had to offer.

Most importantly, a new level of consumerism, increased mobility, and newfound disposable incomes shaped a new kind of human: the teenager, a strange creature that prolonged adolescence and created a liminal space between child and adult. The media of the day, fascinated with the arrival of this new kind of human, speculated that no doubt this quirky behavior exhibited by the young would die out as "they grew up, got proper haircuts and real jobs." Many did, but not without laying the foundations for a new kind of approach to life that would shape the second half of the twentieth century and extend into the twenty-first century. The bohemian lifestyles that Kerouac and the Beat writers had lived on the edges of American culture and that had set the tone for the emergent teen behavior would soon be rocketed into the center of culture as a whole generation sat in the movie house, transfixed by the image of a new kind of rebel, one without a political, social, or religious cause.

HOW JAMES DEAN GOT LOST IN THE UNIVERSE

James Dean's portrayal of Jim Stark, a disaffected teenager struggling to discover a life of meaning in postwar, middle-class suburbia, in the film *Rebel without a Cause*, captured the mood that would soon engulf the youth of the Western world. In the film Jim's parents' marriage is strained. His father fails to offer him a model of masculinity or purpose. Jim finds himself coming of age as the first cracks begin to appear in the previously solid societal understanding of marriage and family.

Jim also models a kind of choice-paralysis in the face of his sexuality. Many critics and observers of the film note the clear sexual subtext in the film. Jim appears to be caught between his heterosexual desires for Judy and his latent homosexual fascination with his friend John "Plato" Crawford, a tension that Dean's biographers have noted as present in the actor's own life. This subtle portrayal of the embryonic teenage sexuality points out a shift from a covenantal ideal of sexuality to one marked by choice, experimentation, and the quest for self-discovery—all themes that would pervade the twenty-first century. Jim's character was the person of the road writ large on the silver screen for the whole of America and indeed the world to see.

It is important to note that *Rebel without a Cause* plays out in the grounds of Griffith Observatory, a shrine to science in the California hills, flanked by saintlike statues of revered scientists such as Galileo, Kepler, Newton, and Copernicus. As Jim watches a presentation on the destruction of the universe, the implication of impending cosmic disaster sets the scene for the morality play that the film becomes. We see unfolding the story of young people coming of age in a culture that provides unparalleled material comfort yet offers a cold vision of life. At the heart of the film is a belief that the universe is empty and purposeless—a spiritual vacuum in which the young must shape their own views of life.

It was this dead vision of material secularism that Kerouac was trying to plot an escape from, one for himself and one for the America he loved. Kerouac would reflect, "In America there is a claw hanging over our brains, which must be pushed aside else it will clutch and strangle our real selves."[8] He noted that what was at stake was not just the place of the Church, or the role of religion in society, but our humanity itself. Jack's writing and whole artistic vision was rooted in the attempt to live an authentic human life in the midst of a secular age.

It was one of those perfect California days when I visited Griffith Observatory. The observatory looked tired and run down. The statues of the scientists were still there, but now James Dean had joined their ranks, a steel bust of the late actor's head now gracing the grounds. As I drove down from the observatory I stopped at a lookout to take in the sight of Los Angeles. Ludicrously for a weekday, two young women in barely-there bikinis sat on the park bench overlooking the city. It was obvious that these young women were up to more than just tanning, and their display had garnered the desired attention. A middle-aged man leaned over them, begging the girls to be in his movie. From the few words being blown around by the wind I gathered that his movie was of the adult persuasion. I moved away from this impromptu outdoor casting couch to the other side of the lookout. Standing next to me was a couple, from their body language they seemed to be on a first date. Again the wind picked up their conversation, throwing it rudely into my face. For a full ten minutes, the male of the couple tried to impress his obviously bored female companion with excruciating details of his luxury yacht. Soon it was almost as if he was talking to himself, or perhaps to the city of Los Angeles, trying to convince her of his importance.

As the wind picked up again, I spotted it, floating almost stationary in the currents of warm air. It was an eagle, stretching out its wings. Swooping, playing and dancing in the air above Los Angeles. It was one of those transcendent moments when you stand there like a kid again, mouth agape, shocked back into an appreciation of the originality of creation. For five minutes I could not take my eyes off the creature as he performed his aeronautical show. I turned to the couple next to me. The eagle was of no interest to them; instead the man's monologue of seafaring luxury continued unabated. The two girls also had failed to notice the bird Instead their eyes, filled with the boredom of modern life, looked over their semi-naked bodies, checking for imperfections. The middle-aged man had now finished his pitch and stared goofily at the girls with a grin that inhabited the ground between cheesy and sleazy. These people were not looking for transcendence, for sublime moments when the divine hand behind creation was revealed. Instead they were lost souls, on the road, looking for meaning in a secular world.

IT WAS ONE OF THOSE TRANSCENDENT MOMENTS WHEN YOU STAND THERE LIKE A KID AGAIN, MOUTH AGAPE, SHOCKED BACK INTO AN APPRECIATION OF THE ORIGINALITY OF CREATION.

SIX:
AN IMMANENT WORLD

The young man holds his broken jaw as blood gushes out onto the pavement. Stunned by the violent attack he has sustained, he struggles to get to his feet. A passerby stops and helps the injured man to his feet. The passerby leans in, seemingly inquiring of the injured man's well-being. This image instantly conjures in our minds echoes of the story of the Good Samaritan. In a second those images of grace and hospitality are vanquished as the passerby reaches into the injured man's bag and robs the victim at his most vulnerable moment. The passerby then walks off with an arrogant and shameless swagger. This moment captured by CCTV was just one of many images of the riots that broke out across the United Kingdom and shocked the world. The riots initially broke out in response to the police shooting of a suspected drug dealer, yet soon spread, lubricated by social media. At first the perpetrators were disenfranchised youth from London's poorer neighborhoods. Soon, however, middle- and upper-class young people joined in the mayhem.

WHY UNDERSTANDING SECULARISM IS THE KEY
TO UNDERSTANDING WHY WE ACT THE WAY WE DO

In the aftermath of the riots commentators and pundits on both sides of politics looked for the causes of the violence and vandalism. The left pointed at the systemic issues, such as poverty, racism, and a lack of education and opportunity. The right in turn pointed the finger at a societal lack of morality and manners. For conservatives the riots were the result of a generation caught in welfare dependency, violent youth with a destructive sense of entitlement. Yet as debate raged, as the public demanded action from the politicians, most missed the deeper cause fueling the riots. The outbreak of destruction was just the symptom of a deeper crisis: a crisis of secularism.

The young people who took to the street to ransack and destroy were living out the worldview of a culture which told them that there was no greater meaning in the world. The riots were a cry from the heart of a secular culture. This was a generation who had grown up in broken families, who had suffered sexual, emotional, and physical abuse; a generation who did not understand home as a place of security. Who had been marginalized by a political system that reduced individuals to mere statistics, who had been raised on a diet of junk food and junk TV. Who lived in a broken world of single-shooter video games, violent hip-hop, and hardcore pornography. A generation who binged on alcohol, lost themselves in drugs, and treated sex as a throwaway commodity because they had been raised in a worldview which implicitly told them life was a cosmic joke.

In this secular desert of meaning, the only hope of transcendence on offer was a new pair of sneakers, a stolen BlackBerry, or the thrill that comes with the sound of smashing glass. Throughout history young people have rioted, thrown off the shackles of oppression, and headed to the palace to overthrow the king. Yet the UK rioters did not head to the houses of Parliament to instigate a new political order. Instead they headed to the stores, stealing what they had been taught was most valuable by their culture. What spilled out on the streets across the United Kingdom during the riots was not just violence, but an abject lack of grace, respect, and hospitality. The robbery of the young Malaysian man showed the world the endgame of the secular worldview—a world in which nothing and no one are sacred.

THE IDIOT'S GUIDE TO SECULARISM

While reams have been written on social change, on postmodernity and generational theory by Christian writers, surprisingly few have tackled the role that the secular plays in shaping our lives. Therefore we must wrestle with an understanding of the idea of the secular. Religious sociologists who spend their lives discussing secularism don't agree fully on a clear definition of the term. The Canadian philosopher Charles Taylor wrestles with the idea of secularism in his book *A Secular Age*. Taylor describes in detail the shift in the West from being an overwhelmingly religious culture in the year fifteen hundred, where it was almost impossible to not believe in God, to our current day in which even the most religious feel the pressure against belief from our secular society. Taylor takes 874 dense and masterful pages to describe this change. I am going to attempt to do something similar in only a few. Inevitably such a short summary will fall short, but it is essential that we understand the context out of which the person of the road was born.

WHY IT USED TO ALMOST BE IMPOSSIBLE
NOT TO BELIEVE IN GOD

The average Joe or Mary of the year 1500 would most likely be a peasant tilling the land. They lived in a culture in which there was no real separation between what we understand as the spiritual and the sacred. The world they inhabited could be described as enchanted. Let me explain. Let's say medieval Joe wants to go on the road. Let's say to visit his aunt in another village twenty miles away. Today if we were going to plan for such a trip our preparation would ensure that our GPS had the right address programmed in, that the car had enough fuel, and that we would know the location of where to stop for a coffee on route. All of our considerations would be practical.

Medieval Joe would also have similar practical concerns. He would not be worried about automobile collisions, but instead about bandits, bears, and the Black Death. Equally worrying would be the inevitable spirits, demons, curses, and various forces of darkness that Joe might encounter on such a trip away from the safety and familiarity of home.

Joe and most likely other members of his village would pray to God fervently for safe passage on what would have been perceived as a spiritually dangerous journey. Such fervency was essential to the medieval Christian who felt completely besieged and surrounded by dark spiritual forces. God and the Christian faith acted like a defensive stronghold, keeping the believers safe inside and the spiritual forces of darkness outside and from completely overrunning the world.

If medieval Joe decided no longer to pray, to worship, or even to believe, he would not be seen as simply exercising his individual religious rights. Instead he would be seen as putting himself, his family, his community, his people, and the whole of Christendom in danger. Such an act of disbelief would be viewed as akin to letting the forces of darkness through the gates to storm the cowering masses inside.

The medieval period was a time of great upheaval. Wars were constant, Islamic forces threatened from the south, the plague killed somewhere between 40 and 50 percent of the population of Europe. Thus its citizens felt that cataclysm could strike at any time. According to the medieval mind the spiritual integrity of Christendom demanded protection and thus vigilance.[1] Therefore the overwhelming social pressure was to believe. Disbelief was viewed at best as treasonous and at worst cosmically deadly.

THE WHOLE WORLD USED TO BE FILLED WITH MEANING

Such a worldview meant that the medieval Christian lived with a view of the universe where God's hand was everywhere and behind everything. The cosmos was a purposeful and ordered place where every decision held moral significance and morality itself carried cosmic weight. In contrast to our culture in which we often complain about a lack of meaning, the medieval universe was one in which the observation could be made that there was too *much* meaning. Every decision carried weight; every choice could lead to spiritual growth or spiritual corruption. The world was heavy with responsibility. Thus there was an incredible pressure to find and live out a framework that brought moral and spiritual order.

To medieval Joe, our contemporary secular world would have seemed unimaginable. For Joe it was almost impossible not to believe, his culture demanded belief. He would have viewed the world as a spiritually dynamic place, overflowing with meaning. The universe was an ordered system which reflected the design of God at every level. Our contemporary rugged individualism would have baffled Joe; our desire for freedom and autonomy would be to him nonsensical and frightening. Joe would have seen himself simply as a very small player in a much larger cosmic drama orchestrated by God. Sure he might go on a religious pilgrimage, but medieval Joe did not need to go on the road in a search for meaning: he was already drowning in it.

WHY JACK KEROUAC CRIED IN CHURCH

Kerouac stood in the human beehive that is Grand Central Station. He wanted a place to sit and reflect on his life but could find no place amongst the bustle. He would lament, "All there was —marble floor, rushing crowds, dime lockers, bleak seatless spaces and bright vast spaces. What a thing men have let themselves in for, in this New York!—so big that it is utterly impossible."[2] Kerouac fled up Fifth Avenue, ignoring the storefronts with their displays; cutting through the freezing streets he sought refuge in St. Patrick's Cathedral. The church sat across the street from its secular rival, a large department store. As Kerouac sat in silence and prayer, he discovered the everyday worries and thoughts that had been plaguing him dropped away, and his focus moved to God. To him the cathedral was not just a place of sanctuary; it was a remnant of a lost world:

> Such lovely silence; such heights of mysterious upreaching darkness. . . . I could hear . . . the faint roar of New York traffic without. I looked up to see the blue light of evening on the night windows, and I thought, "If it was only 500 years ago, and in Stuttgart, and I could [go] up to my sacristy and write my devotional hymns and ring the bell! . . . The whole weight of medieval scholarship was behind it; the unbelievable labours of thousands of impoverished artisans and mere amateur laborers; the grand inspiration of men like . . . Bach."[3]

The medieval age of Christianity was gone; St. Patrick's was a rare island in the ocean of secular power that is Manhattan. "Outside, it was the tremendous, awful walls of Manhattan skyscrapers. Oh, what an evil world was outside, and what a really evil world it is . . . Frankly . . . I don't know when it happened; when it was that I began almost crying."[4] Kerouac was mourning the loss of the Christian world, which was being subsumed by the postwar culture. The world was secularizing—it was becoming disenchanted.

HOW OUR WORLD LOST ITS SENSE OF MEANING

So how did the world in which medieval Joe once lived become disenchanted? How did we go from a culture that demanded belief of us to one where belief is marginalized, barely tolerated, or even mocked? The secularism with which we live was born out of revulsion with the religious wars that ravaged Europe between the sixteenth and seventeenth centuries. These conflicts were a result of the Reformation in which Protestantism broke away from the Catholic Church. After the bloodshed, key thinkers began to believe that if religion could be removed from the public sphere, then the religious motives for war would disappear, and society could enjoy peace. In the new pluralistic religious landscape, passionate forms of faith were seen as divisive. Charles Taylor notes, "From the eighteenth century . . . we see a reaction which identifies in a strongly transcendent version of Christianity a danger for the goods of the modern moral order."[5]

Michael Allen Gillespie believes that secularism is at the very core of our modern culture, that in the West the worldview is "a result of the displacement of religious belief from its position of prominence at the center of public life into a private realm where it could be freely practiced as long as it did not challenge secular authority, science, or reason. The authority of religion to shape private and public life thus was replaced by a notion of private belief and ultimately personal 'values.'"[6]

Faith, spirituality, and religion are tolerated if they stay in the confines of the private sphere, be it the home, the religious school, or a place of worship. But our economic, social, recreational, political, physical, and educational lives tend to be lived in the public square. Thus the person of the road, whether believer or unbeliever, lives the whole of or at least a majority of their everyday life as a practical atheist. That is, although they may in their minds believe in God, they act for large parts of their waking life as if He does not exist.

And our lives have become disenchanted for another reason.

A SLEEK, COMFORTABLE, YET MEANINGLESS WORLD

It is a frigid, dark night and a suffocating fear comes over me. It is intense and overwhelming. I ring my wife but I cannot get through. My hosts had dropped me off six hours earlier, they will return to pick me up for a day of speaking in the morning. I look around the luxurious hotel room, it is sleek and modern, filled with smooth surfaces and minimalist design. I move to the window and look out across the curve of the building and the masses of other hotel rooms. Only three lonely lights burn. The large-screen TV has countless programs to watch but nothing that interests me. I had forgotten to pack my Bible, so I open the drawer, looking for the obligatory Gideon Bible. The drawer yawns emptily back at me. I walk around the room opening every cupboard and crevice but there is no Bible. I grab my jacket and key and head out the door. As I walk down the corridor I try to listen for sounds of life from the other rooms, but there is only silence. As I wait for the lift I stare at a black-and-white photograph framed on the wall. It features some rocks in a riverbed. It seems unnatural, a slice of creation extracted, de-colorized, and reduced.

As I ride the elevator down to the ground floor I try to think of conversations that I can engage the concierge in. Yet as the doors of the elevator open, the lobby is completely empty. I stand at the desk waiting for the concierge to emerge. I stand there for ten minutes, no one appears. Under my breath I crack a joke, "What is this? The hotel from *The Shining*?" No one is there to hear nor laugh. I head out into the street. The hotel is part of a whole urban development. Attached to the hotel are restaurants, parks, stores, and apartments. The contemporary design of the hotel is maintained throughout the whole development. No doubt as the urban planner presented his plans, the parks and walkways would have been filled with images of people, yet tonight here

JUST LIKE THE SECULAR ARCHITECTS OF OUR CULTURE, THE ARCHITECT OF THIS HOTEL DEVELOPMENT HAS PLANNED FOR EVERYTHING EXCEPT FOR GOD.

in real life, the streets are empty. The restaurants are shut, the apartments have no lights on, the park is only inhabited by a biting wind. I stand in the middle of the road, there are no cars. I walk around for ten minutes, I do not see a car nor a soul. Then I spot a light emanating from a kebab shop. I head in and order, trying to strike up a conversation with the man behind the counter. He does not seem interested and instead stares out the window seeming bored witless. I take my kebab and head back to my room. The garlic sauce drips from my meal onto the glass table. I leave it there, its messiness a comfort, a reminder of life amongst the cold surfaces. A sense of cosmic loneliness overtakes me. I realize that the hotel room, the hotel, and the whole development is a metaphor for our secular culture. It is well designed, comfortable, filled with every mod con that the contemporary person could want. Yet it is soulless. It is designed for living but not for life. The smoothness of the surfaces reveals a lack of depth, the Scandinavian minimalism reveals a minimalist worldview. Just like the secular architects of our culture, the architect of this hotel development has planned for everything except for God.

WHY WE ONLY BELIEVE WHAT WE CAN SEE AND FEEL

The rise of natural science has also heavily contributed to the secularization of our lives. Many have noted that Christianity gave birth to science. Rooted in a belief that God had created an ordered world, science laid the intellectual foundations to then explore, measure, and understand that world. Scientists such as Newton, Galileo, and Copernicus were believers. Yet over time a new form of natural science, also known as naturalism, began to take precedence.

Naturalism—also known as materialism—perceives reality as only matter. The ultimate authority in this worldview is scientific measurement. In more simple terms: *If we can't see it, it ain't there.* Therefore for the adherent of naturalism, all that exists is nature. This philosophy helped destroy the enchanted view of the world that medieval Joe would have possessed. Theologian Terence Nichols explains that the philosophy of naturalism began with "the separation of God from nature, a split that began in the late medieval and early modern period. This resulted in the (perceived) separation of God from everyday life that is so characteristic of contemporary secular societies. The main carrier of this has been modern natural science. Science came to understand nature as a mechanical system that operated more or less independently from God. God was thus gradually (over centuries) removed from the cosmos."[7]

The effects of such a change were immense. Faith in God was shifting to faith in humanity. Historian Frederick L. Nussbaum comments, "Faith in man's power to know and to understand operated powerfully to turn men's hopes and interests from religion to science."[8]

There was a new sheriff in town. When a culture comes to believe that all there is is nature and matter, it will stop looking to clergy, the Church, and Holy Scripture for guidance. The mystical, the spiritual, and the religious in such a worldview are deemed irrelevant and marginalized. Nichols continues, "This sense pervades the cultures of the developed West, including American culture. It is this that makes the practice of Christianity in everyday life so difficult, especially for young people, who grow up enchanted by the secular media."[9] In such a worldview the religious are seen as people who live in a fantasy. Like moviegoers who suspend their disbelief when they enter the cinema, the religious are seen as doing the same when they enter spaces of worship.

> LIKE MOVIEGOERS WHO SUSPEND THEIR DISBELIEF WHEN THEY ENTER THE CINEMA, THE RELIGIOUS ARE SEEN AS DOING THE SAME WHEN THEY ENTER SPACES OF WORSHIP.

As we have learned, for medieval Joe it was almost impossible not to believe. We, however, find ourselves in the opposite position: the weight of culture pushes against our belief. Belief is now a countercultural act of rebellion.

No longer then is faith a social compass, something which informs the whole of life, explains the cosmos, and offers meaning. Religion's function in the contemporary West is radically altered, as Craig M. Gay explains: "Religion has thus forfeited its role as the interpreter of social order and has become instead a matter of personal preference and choice, something to be adopted and/or discarded privately as each of us sees fit."[10] Faith then morphs into something personal, sentimental, and therapeutic.

WHAT THE ALMOST-FROZEN BODY OF A DEAD FRENCH GUY TAUGHT ME ABOUT FAITH

As I walk through the early morning streets of France's ancient capital of Tours, I can feel the cobblestones pressing through the soles of my sneakers. I pull the collar of my jacket up in a vain attempt to keep out the cold. The church known as the Basilique de St. Martin rises up above the shops and houses. The church contains the remains of St. Martin, a third-century missionary to France. Martin was born in modern-day Hungary and is best known for evangelizing the Gallic tribes in the fourth century. Without men like Martin, Christianity would never have gained a foothold within pagan Europe. I enter the church and notice the temperature drop significantly. This fact does not seem to affect the few solitary souls at early morning prayers. I look up into the heights of the chapel built to push the eye upward in contemplation of a transcendent God.

The history of this particular church is intertwined with the fate of Christianity in Europe. The first church built on this site was burned down at the turn of the first millennium. In the thirteenth century at the height of the Church's power in Europe a grand Romanesque basilica was built on the site, becoming a popular place of pilgrimage. During the Reformation, French Protestants ransacked the church, attacking Martin's grave. The church would eventually be fully destroyed during the French Revolution, as the revolutionaries attempted to expunge faith from the new established Republic. The smaller church I am standing in was rebuilt during the nineteenth century. I head downward into the belly of the church. As I descend the stairs into Martin's crypt I feel a noticeable drop in the temperature. It feels like a meat locker. I stand in the small room and stare at Martin's resting place. Here in the cold room, it feels as if underneath secular France, this memory of

Europe's Christian past is frozen, lying dormant.

I head up the stairs, out of the church and onto the street. In the street outside, the shops were beginning to start their trade for the day. The pilgrims no longer flocked to St. Martin's grave; the stores were now the holy sites. Secularism had flowed out of France across the world. Like a cosmic steamroller it had flattened the world, removed the transcendent, and compressed the sacred into a few hours a week, only accessed by the truly devoted. The wildness of belief was now contained—hidden, like St. Martin, underneath the surface. To discover the transcendent one must now search for it. The steamroller makes the ground ready for the road.

Back to Jack Kerouac. Faced with the secular towers of Manhattan, repelled by his culture, by what his America has become. Jack feels the lure of the road. He is over his friends, who are lost in a kind of European existential crisis. He is sick of their theories, their intellectualism, and their coldness. In contrast to the freezing, claustrophobic streets of New York, Jack dreams of the warmth and expanse of the highway. So Jack sets off on his quasi-religious, quasi-hedonistic journey. Drawn by the lure of the road, to chart out the journey that will be followed by millions to come who search for meaning in the secular world. Jack would attempt to carve out a life of meaning within a culture that saw life as immanent.

SEVEN:
CARVING OUT A LIFE
OF MEANING

A culture which sees faith as something personal and divorced from everyday life, which sees reality as limited to nature and matter, can be described as one which has an immanent view of the world. That is to say that it believes that reality is enclosed within nature and that there is nothing outside of it. In contrast, Christian faith believes in the transcendent, that there are key elements of life beyond nature. That all that exists is not simply contained in what we can sense and measure. Historical Christianity can be described as a faith which believes in a transcendent God who is beyond and exists apart from the cosmos and nature. Secular culture's immanence demands us to live within a very narrow view of the world and of reality. The secular cosmos is a reduced one, one devoid of the transcendent. It is this immanent view of the world that sends the citizens of the West on to the road in search of the transcendent.

HOW WE CAME TO BELIEVE THAT NOTHING REALLY MATTERS

What does it mean to live in a place of no moral significance? Sociologists Christian Smith and Melinda Lundquist Denton explain the implications:

> When a person lives in a morally insignificant universe . . . there is no natural law or world-historic struggles and achievements. When one looks up into the stars, one sees not the gods, nor the handiwork of God, nor the portentous alignment of planets; one simply sees empty space in which nobody else is at home. People living in such a universe find themselves in a small corner of that empty space of which their short lives have come by chance and for reasons nonexistent into being on this minor and insignificant bit of carbon floating in a galaxy destined for extinction. There is no Creator who set humanity here and guides our lives and history with providence. There is no larger law-like order in nature that structures the moral living of the human race. . . . There is no judgment, no final retribution or punishment, not even a remembrance of one's life or anything human after time and physics have run their course. There is . . . simply the given self and world and experience. Nothing more.[1]

To hold to an immanent view of the world is to believe there are only atoms. There is nothing after death, nothing beyond the universe. Life is a cosmic fluke. Humans are simply bipeds. The death of millions of starving Africans is helpful population control. The love a parent feels for their child is nothing more than a genetic impulse to continue the species. Love for a spouse is nothing more than pheromones and oxytocin. The Himalayas are not majestic and awe-inspiring, they are just big rocks. Literature is simply typing, and art is a joke. Everything you feel, everything you hold to passionately, is simply neurons, and sparks of electricity in the brain of a naked ape. All of our human activity is ultimately meaningless, the scratching around of a virulent species of animals in their denial of their eventually cold and lonely deaths. Within the immanent frame, your life does not matter one cosmic iota.

Yet we want our lives to matter. People travel, change jobs, crave love, seek experiences, act heroically, create, sculpt, and shape their lives in a quest of meaning. As humans we are wired for the transcendent. We desire moments which will take our breath away, we feel stung by pain and robbed by death, we hunger after mystery. Yet immanent, secular culture tells us that this is all there is. Our culture's jettisoning of faith and embrace of the immanent comes at a terrible personal cost, as historians Will and Ariel Durant diagnose, saying that the "decline of religious belief [led to] the pessimism that would be the secret malady of the modern soul."[2]

WE DESIRE MOMENTS WHICH WILL TAKE OUR BREATH AWAY, WE FEEL STUNG BY PAIN AND ROBBED BY DEATH, WE HUNGER AFTER MYSTERY.

The horror of a godless culture would reverberate around the West in the nineteenth and twentieth centuries. Nothing captures this sense of desperation and loss more than Norwegian artist Edvard Munch's painting—a series of paintings, actually—known as *The Scream*. The work is one of the most recognized in the world, vividly illustrating the angst and alienation of the modern soul. The strange figure emitting the scream was thought by art critic Robert Rosenblum to have been inspired by a Peruvian mummy seen by Munch at a Paris exhibition[3] and thus offers the commentary that modern humans were mummifying in a reduced universe. Munch wrote of the painting:

> I was walking along a path with two friends—the sun was setting—suddenly the sky turned blood red. I paused, feeling

exhausted, and leaned on the fence—there was blood and tongues of fire above the blue-black fjord and the city. My friends walked on, and I stood there trembling with anxiety— and I sensed an infinite scream passing through nature."[4]

> **MY FRIENDS WALKED ON, AND I STOOD THERE TREMBLING WITH ANXIETY—AND I SENSED AN INFINITE SCREAM PASSING THROUGH NATURE.**

The anxiety that Munch spoke of was to become emblematic of the modern age. With no God there was no moral order, and the thought of living in a purely immanent world was horrifying—and thus a scream passed through nature. One that many were only too happy to ignore.

Many, but not a certain melancholic and mustachioed Prussian philosopher. If Kerouac had shown us the way to the road, this philosopher built the road.

HOW A GERMAN GUY WITH A MUSTACHE MADE US BELIEVE THAT NOTHING REALLY MATTERS

At the beginning of *On the Road,* Kerouac writes that Dean Moriarty (Neal Cassady) wishes to learn about Friedrich Nietzsche. This mention of the long-dead philosopher comes on the first page of *On the Road*, marking the influence that Nietzsche had over the postwar social and spiritual malaise that Kerouac was trying to find a way out of. Commenting on the legacy of Nietzsche, Peter Gay says, "More than anyone else, he provided his world with the climate for modernism."[5] While Nietzsche's nineteenth-century intellectual peers had subscribed to the immanent worldview with its eclipse of religion, very few seemed to want to live out the implications of their lack of belief. The middle classes still saw themselves as religious, yet to Nietzsche they lived secular everyday lives. "They feel themselves already fully occupied, these good people, be it by their businesses or by their pleasures . . . it seems that they have no time whatever left for religion."[6]

Nietzsche saw such contradictory behavior as hypocritical. Thus his most famous statement "God is dead" was as much a theological statement as it was a sociological one. Western culture acted secularly even if it did not want to own up to this fact.

When Nietzsche proclaimed the death of God, he was, in the words of David Wells, "speaking of the passing of a world in which meaning and values had been rooted in the transcendent."[7] In the view of Nietzsche, the citizens of the West had to accept that they lived in an immanent, secular culture. They could not sentimentally hold to Christian morals such as ideas of justice and equality. Jesus was not coming back to save anyone. Humans were alone; the entire hope of salvation was now dead. All that was left was the quest for individual authenticity. In the words of Richard Tarnas, "To be authentic one had to admit, and choose freely to encounter, the stark reality of life's meaninglessness."[8] Here are the seeds of the life script lived by so many today. Gone were transcendent, God-given senses of purpose and meaning; instead:

> The individual had to create their own concepts of meaning. There were no longer ultimate values but only present possibilities — possibilities that were fluid, open, and unstructured by the divine or by an absolute moral order. This is the world that we describe under the rubric of secularization.[9]

Nietzsche believed that with no God, humans themselves must become godlike shapers of reality. He was no misty-eyed New Ager, expecting humanity to evolve to a spiritual plane. Nietzsche understood that in the immanent world, only the strong would now survive. Love and compassion were Christian sentimentalities. Power was all that counted. A secular world was ripe for conquest by powerful men (*ubermensch*), who by the sheer force of their wills would dominate. The problem with the world according to Nietzsche was not evil but weakness. Nietzsche despised the weak, the disabled, and the elderly. He would advise doctors that

> A sick person is a parasite on society. Once one has reached a certain state it is indecent to live any longer. Vegetating on in cowardly dependence on physicians and their methods, once the meaning of life, the right to life has been lost, should be greeted with society's profound contempt. The physicians, for their part, ought to convey this contempt—not prescriptions, but every day a fresh dose of disgust at their patient.[10]

Nietzsche would also turn his scorn on women, the humble, and the broken, and would advocate the sacrifice of the poor to the rich in his book *Beyond Good and Evil*.

You don't have to be a history major to see the influence that his thought would have on the coming Nazi Third Reich. Hitler ordered that his troops be given copies of Nietzsche's books as they went into battle.

In our contemporary culture in which a comment that even hints of prejudice by a media personality can result in scorn and career suicide, it is unimaginable that such a philosopher is studied, vaunted, and not scorned and his books banned. Part of the reason that Nietzsche's influence is still so profound is that his charges against us still ring true. On one hand we advocate an equal and just society in which no one is discriminated against because of race, creed, or gender. We hope that the elderly and the disabled are treated with dignity and respect, we wish for a day when the poor and the starving of the world will be fed, when wars will end and peace will reign.

Yet I believe if he was alive, Nietzsche would point at our

television screens full of the healthy, beautiful, and young, at our sports that elevate and laud the muscular, at our politics that reward the strong and the powerful. He would force us to look at our culture of real and passive aggression in which individuals compete against each other in a battle of wills, in the home, in the markets, and the workplace. His face would redden, his veins would pop and spittle would catch in his mustache, as Nietzsche, screaming in exasperation, would point out our elderly homes, our abortion clinics, our battlefields, our refugee camps, and the starving millions of the two-thirds world. Nietzsche would call us hypocrites as he laughed at our claims of being a society of freedom, justice, compassion, and tolerance.

His ghost still haunts us because beneath our veneer of sentimentality, in everyday life we practice his brand of nihilism. He reminds us that there is a dark side to the culture of the road. By living within the immanent frame we unwittingly make ourselves his disciples. Each of us, atheist, believer, or agnostic, operates from a Nietzschean playbook for huge swaths of our everyday lives. We try through a force of will to shape our lives, to suit our dreams, our desires, and our wants. To make it happen on our terms. The road becomes the arena in which we strive to exert our wills on the world.

Ironically, considering his disdain for the mentally ill, on January 3, 1889, in Turin, Italy, Nietzsche fell into a mental collapse from which he would never recover. One could almost say that Nietzsche's fate mirrored the collapse into insanity that Western culture would experience over the coming century. The triumph of the immanent worldview and the removal of a Christian ethic from the minds of many would lead directly to the doors of the Nazi concentration camp and the Soviet gulag. With religion marginalized and its cultural effect made impotent, the State takes over.

The existential horror of this period would inspire George Orwell in 1949 to write his classic dystopian novel *1984,* painting a godless future where the individual lived in a world disenchanted beyond recognition—a world which Kerouac hoped to re-enchant by taking to the road.

WHERE IS AMERICA GOING IN HER SHINY CAR?

Midway through *On the Road*, Sal and Neal decide to embark upon a road trip. Carlo Marx questions their motives for heading off on another seemingly pointless trip. "What is the meaning of this voyage to New York? What kind of sordid business are you on now? I mean, man, whither goest thou? Whither goest thou? Whither goest thou, America, in thy shiny car in the night?"[11] Marx is not just questioning Sal and Neal but the whole restlessness and striving of postwar American culture, made even easier by the mobility of the motor car.

Neal and Sal have no answer for Marx's line of questioning. "We sat and didn't know what to say; there was nothing to talk about anymore. The only thing to do was to go."[12] To move is normal. Ironically Sal and Dean are caught in the rootlessness of the immanent world they so despise. As the duo arrives in New York, Neal has had a kind of religious epiphany during their travels, ranting excitedly to Sal, "And of course now no one can tell us that there is no God. . . . You remember, Sal, when I first came to New York and I wanted Chad King to teach about Nietzsche. You see how long ago? Everything is fine, God exists."[13]

On one hand Sal and Neal are rejecting the immanent culture. Neal no longer wants to learn about Nietzsche and his declaration that God is dead. Neal's travels on the road have confirmed to him that God is indeed alive and present in modern America.

Yet Neal and Sal's mobility, their hunger for experience, their questing, and their hedonistic appetite show all the hallmarks of a Nietzschean framework. They want God, they hunger for the spiritual and for meaning. They recognize that their culture is bereft of the transcendent. Yet they also revel in the personal freedom that the immanent frame brings. They want holy rantings, epiphanies, and divine revelations. They want the enchanted world back.

Yet at the same time, they desire no authority, no external moral codes. They want Christ, but they also want the girls and the drugs. They want the solace of God and meaning, but also the freedom of godlessness. It is this tension that is at the heart of the culture of the road. It will also define the decade to come—the sixties.

EIGHT:
THE SIXTIES

When Kerouac was writing *On the Road*, he and his friends were simply a group of bohemians and lowlifes, living on the edge of American culture. As the Beats slowly began to be published, the media began to listen to this strange group. The first half of the twentieth century had been defined by political radicals, be they anarchists, socialists, fascists, or communists. However, Kerouac and the Beats were a different kind of radical. As Kerouac's moniker Beat was applied to his generation, media outlets gobbled up this descriptor and filled magazines and newspapers with stories of the group's avant-garde lifestyles.

WHY CHURCH ATTENDANCE FLATLINED IN THE SIXTIES

Suddenly to be Beat or a beatnik was hip. Network TV introduced a beatnik character, Maynard G. Krebs, played by Bob Denver, into the series *The Many Loves of Dobie Gillis*. In cartoons and movies, beatniks became ubiquitous in their berets, black sweaters, and sandals, carrying the obligatory pair of bongos. *Playboy* would even feature a centerfold dressed as a beatnik. This turn would send Kerouac into a depression. His vision for the re-enchantment of America was turning into a pop culture joke. A misreading of his work, one that would define his literary career, was just beginning.

Many of the teens who had identified with Jim Stark in *Rebel without a Cause* were now reluctantly entering adulthood, and would find a similar sympathy and inspiration in Kerouac's characters of Sal and Neal. Kerouac awoke to find himself a cult icon, a symbol of a youthful new generation determined to dramatically change American culture. To his tremendous displeasure he was sought out by the media as a spokesman for a generation. Inspired by his books, kids would start turning up at his door, seeking him out, often shocked that he was not the twentysomething hitting the road that they imagined. Instead Jack was a tired and increasingly disillusioned man on the wrong side of thirty-five. The fans seemed to forget that Jack was the author; he was not Dean Moriarty. As the societal changes that would blow up into the sixties counterculture were emerging, Kerouac would write:

> To think that I had so much to do with it . . . and I was already sick of the whole subject. Nothing can be more dreary than "coolness" . . . postured, actually secretly rigid coolness that covers up the fact that the character is unable to convey anything of force or interest, a kind of sociological coolness soon to become a fad up into the mass of middleclass youth. . . . All this was about to sprout out all over America even down to high school level and be attributed in part to my doing!"[1]

Kerouac would grow more disenchanted with the rucksack revolution that he had earlier called for: as the sixties became more liberal, he would become more conservative. But let's not get too far ahead of ourselves.

The sixties are crucial at this juncture of our exploration. The decade sees the convergence of a number of spot fires into a raging inferno that radically changes the concept of personhood in the West. The war in Vietnam rocks confidence in both government and the solidity of institutions. The women's movement, the civil rights movement, the environmental movement, and the antiwar movement effect an entire rethinking of the West's cultural past, casting a veil of suspicion over the role of the Church and any previously held "established" or "traditional" moral and social values or frameworks. The invention and proliferation of the contraceptive pill caps off a host of fundamental changes in the way sexuality is viewed outside of the previously held model of Christian marital covenantality.

Change was in the air—yes, political change, but also personal change. All kinds of rules and taboos were being broken; uncharted ground was being trod upon. "Sixties radicals needed a new scripture to justify their creed, and they found it in . . . *On the Road*,"[2] reflects theologian Stephen H. Webb. Kerouac's book had reached its time, seemingly charting a way forward for a generation that was truly modern.

HOW THE BEATLES (SORT OF) KILLED THE CHURCH

In his study of Christianity in Britain, Callum Brown notes that it was the sixties that saw the real decline of the Church, particularly its evangelical wing. Fascinatingly Brown records that decline occurs quite suddenly in 1963, noting this decline occurred at the same time as the release of the Beatles' first LP prophetically titled *Please, Please Me*—words that would capture the hedonistic individualism that was to come. The accompanying Beatlemania seemed almost ecstatically religious in nature. The sight of young women, screaming and writhing, must have seemed deeply shocking to British culture, still somewhat moored in Victorian propriety. Tellingly, 1963 was the year that the first postwar baby boomers hit eighteen and legal adulthood. Brown writes:

> The generation that grew up in the sixties was more dissimilar to the generation of its parents than in any previous century. . . . The range of the changes in demography, personal relationships, political debate and moral concerns was so enormous that it did not so much challenge the Christian churches as bypass them.[3]

No longer did the Christian story shape the inner world of the West. Two thousand years of Christian culture and discipleship were left behind as the road of personal discovery lay ahead. "It is precisely because 'the personal' changed so much in the 1960s—and has continued to change in the four decades since—that the church is in seemingly terminal decay and British Christian culture is in its death throes."[4]

The Church, reeling from this multiplicity of changes, understandably fails to discern adequately that a new form of personhood has emerged, and thus is unable to respond effectively.

Kerouac's personal errors were to become the errors of the sixties. The inherent contradiction in Kerouac's life and work, a desire for a life of meaning and yet a desire for individual autonomy, would be passed onto the generations to come. Today's Western culture is still mired in the same crisis. The sixties generation, like Kerouac, wished to re-enchant America. Yet they wished to do so without the constrictions of tradition, biblical revelation, and Christian morality. Kerouac's life on the road was not a rejection of his Christian heritage but an attempt to reengineer it.

NINE:
THE CALIFORNIA SELF

I am standing in the heart of America, almost exactly in the middle. There is a frost on the grass. The sun cuts through the cold of the morning. I am engaged in that most American of experiences, making my way to Walmart. I cross the large grass field that separates my hotel from the store and stop, looking up into the morning sky. Crisscrossing the blue canvas are the vapor trails of countless commercial jets, heading both westward and eastward. Each white line in the atmosphere seems to say to me that where I am is inadequate. I can almost feel palpably the magnetic pull of the coasts.

HOW CALIFORNIA CHANGED THE WORLD

Kerouac understood the mythical pull of the American coasts. With his Catholic roots Kerouac would have also been aware of the Christian tradition of pilgrimage. His book *On the Road*, and all of his traveling books, re-invoke the tradition of pilgrimage in a quasi-secular form. Christians throughout history have traveled to places that are seen as having a dimension of the holy, be it Jerusalem, Rome, or Santiago de Compostela. In his work on pilgrimage, Martin Robinson comments:

> The holy place is seen as a physical location where the membrane between this world and a reality beyond is especially thin, where a transcendent reality impinges on the immanent. The hopeful traveler seeks to meet with the holy as a means of bringing meaning to this life.[1]

The American settlers fleeing religious persecution in the Old World of Europe reframed their migration in the imagery of pilgrimage. America itself was envisioned as a holy space, filled with potential and possibility. As America grew, its cities would be imbued with a symbolic function. Sal and Dean's travels across America illustrate the way that its cities had become secular holy sites. This is equally true today as it was half a century ago. New York, Los Angeles, and Las Vegas are all secular pilgrimage sites, in a way that Chicago, Boston, and Phoenix are not.

Traditionally sites are made holy because they are connected in some way to religious history: they are associated with miracles, visions, radical conversions, or healing, or they are the home or resting place of a saint. New York is revered as a secular holy site to which millions make pilgrimage because it is woven into the history and imagination of our secular scripture—the cinema. Thousands each year take tours around the Big Apple, stopping off for a firsthand encounter with landmarks that were used in popular movies. The hope of the pilgrim is that some of the "movie magic" will rub off onto them. In Los Angeles, you can visit the homes and even graves of celebrities, our contempo-

NEW YORK, LOS ANGELES, AND LAS VEGAS ARE ALL SECULAR PILGRIMAGE SITES, IN A WAY THAT CHICAGO, BOSTON, AND PHOENIX ARE NOT.

rary versions of saints. Both New York and Los Angeles offer the potential of the miracle, not a supernatural miracle, but the secular miracle; the existential healing and the vocational rebirth—be it the girl from a small town who comes to L.A. and is "discovered," "healed" of her obscurity, and who now reaches secular sainthood as a major movie star, or the homeless man who through grit and determination rises from the street to be "reborn" a financial titan of Wall Street.

The hymns of Frank Sinatra and Jay-Z attest to the magical power of the coasts and their symbolic capitals. Artists as diverse as Tupac and the Mamas and the Papas have serenaded New York—sending words of praise toward the West. The mythology of the coasts, the secular aura of New York and Los Angeles, offer a touch of the transcendence to those seeking meaning within the immanent world. They are the canvases for Nietzsche's unwitting followers to paint their worlds with meaning. They are miragelike destinations that hover just over the horizon.

> **THE HYMNS OF FRANK SINATRA AND JAY-Z ATTEST TO THE MAGICAL POWER OF THE COASTS AND THEIR SYMBOLIC CAPITALS.**

WHY NEW YORK WAS KILLING KEROUAC'S SOUL

The East Coast, with its fusion of European and American cultures, was to Kerouac the old world. It also represented to him everything that was wrong with modernity. New York represented power; it was finance, department stores, and skyscrapers. It was home to the publishers, professors, and intellectual elites that Kerouac felt disdain for, who he felt had lost touch with the real America. Yet for Kerouac New York was a cold metropolis that left one horribly lonely. In *On the Road* Sal of the East Coast heads West with Dean, whom he describes with the awe of a young child meeting their cinema cowboy hero: "My first impression of Dean was of a young Gene Autry—trim, thin-hipped, blue-eyed . . . a sideburned hero of the snowy West."[2] The description of Dean makes him seem out of place in the "evil gray New York pad."[3] Sal's New York intellectual friends represent the detached intellectualism that had defined the first half of the twentieth century. Sal says of them, "All my New York friends were in their negative, nightmare position of putting down society and giving their tired bookish or political or psychoanalytical reasons."[4] Kerouac needed rescuing from this intellectual prison.

In contrast was Kerouac's great Western Hero: "Dean just raced in society, eager for bread and love; he didn't care one way or the other, 'so long's I can get that lil ole gal' . . . and 'so long's we can eat, son, y'ear me?'"[5] Dean was symbolic of the half century that was to come, of the move from politics to the personal, from a search for intellectual truth to a quest for individual experience. Dean was an unabashed hedonist. Sal notes, "For him sex was the one and only holy thing in life."[6] Scenes in *On the Road* are harbingers of the sexual revolution that was to come.

Dean is a child of the road. He has grown up around cars, he steals cars for fun, and he works often as a parking attendant, showing off his skill behind the wheel. For Jack, Dean represents a new way of life, a new way of being—a role fulfilled today by the beautiful, virile people who stare out at us from billboards, magazines, movies, and television and beckon us away from the mundane, from responsibility and commitment.

KEROUAC LOOKS FOR GOD, GIRLS, AND DRUGS

Dean explodes into Sal's East Coast reality and beckons him westward toward a new understanding of self. Dean's lifestyle is an "overburst of American joy: it was Western, the west wind . . . something new, long prophesied, long a-coming." Sal is intoxicated at this promise of a new dawn breaking out in the coldness of the postwar secular culture. He cannot resist any longer, despite the warnings of his aunt, who represents faith, convention, and tradition. Sal sets off on the embryonic road trip. He wants God, but he also wants "kicks." "I could hear a new call and see a new horizon. . . . Somewhere along the line I knew there'd be girls, visions, everything; somewhere along the line the pearl would be handed to me. . . . I was ready to go to the West Coast."[7]

Sal takes off on a journey westward, a journey that thousands of other Americans had taken a decade earlier during the great Dust Bowl disaster in search of a better life for their families, a migration immortalized in John Steinbeck's novel *The Grapes of Wrath*. Sal, however, is not a refugee from an economic calamity, in search of work. Instead he is heading West, fleeing convention, trying to eke out a sense of meaning in an immanent world. Sal is following his guide Dean westward on the road.

THE GURU ON A SEGWAY

As the coffee combines with the Californian sunshine, my jet lag begins to disappear. I watch the traffic fly by as people scurry to work with their obligatory white earbuds firmly stuck in their ears. A homeless man scans the garbage cans for anything of worth. Across the street is a New Age center. The signs in its windows promise all kinds of metaphysical goodies. There are classes in yoga, tantric sex, and life coaching. Out of the door of the center comes the strangest sight: a large middle-aged man, wearing Gandhi-style Dhoti pants. This traditional Indian dress is matched with a singlet complete with food stains that I can spot from across the street. The man kind of looks like Santa Claus with his white beard, yet he has his hair tied up in a samurai-style topknot. The most unusual thing is his mode of transport, however—the guru is riding a Segway. I think to myself, "Only in California."

Since Americans started heading westward, the West Coast had always held an allure deep within the American psyche. The West, in particular California, was viewed mythologically. A place of potential, of fluidity, lawless yet filled with possibilities. At first its allure was sun and farming, then gold, then its attractions became Hollywood, Disneyland, and fame. Behind each of these lures was a promise of freedom, a forgetting of the past, the appeal of personal reinvention. Nathaniel West explored the lure of the West in his 1925 novel *The Day of the Locust*. West saw California as a second chance at Eden, one character exclaiming, "Why, it's a paradise on earth!"[8] In West's novel, California is a place where its citizens reinvent themselves superficially:

> A great many of the people wore sports clothes which were not really sports clothes. Their sweaters, knickers, slacks, blue flannel jackets with brass buttons were fancy dress. The fat lady in the yachting cap was going shopping, not boating; the man in the Norfolk jacket and Tyrolean hat was returning, not from a mountain, but an insurance office; and the girl in slacks and sneaks with a bandanna around her head had just left a switchboard, not a tennis court.[9]

The clothes act as masks, totally disconnected from the true identities or histories of their wearers. West also notes scathingly that the same disconnectedness could be applied to Californian architecture:

> But not even the soft wash of dusk could help the houses. Only dynamite would be of any use against the Mexican ranch houses, Samoan huts, Mediterranean villas, Egyptian and Japanese temples, Swiss chalets, Tudor cottages, and every possible combination of these styles that lined the slopes of the canyon.[10]

In California, Hollywood and the age of the image was dawning. With no authority outside to look to, the self could re-mold itself however it chose. The person of the road had complete freedom to choose who it was to be.

WHY WE ARE ALL CALIFORNIANS NOW

After reading *The Day of the Locust* and its critique of Californian life, the poet W. H. Auden coined the term "West's disease" to illustrate the particular spiritual poverty emanating out of California—a poverty born out of a frustration, when one's desires were not transformed into wishes. Psychologist Martin Seligman would also use the symbolism of the American coasts to describe the radical shift in our understanding of self which would give birth to the culture of the road. Seligman would name it New England Self, a sense of self which would mark the first half of the twentieth century. The New England Self is religious, traditional, hardworking, puts others, community, and family over self, and values commitment over personal pleasure. In contrast is the California Self, which comes to dominate the second half of the century. The California Self fits perfectly with the worldview of the road. Commenting on Seligman's definition, John F. Schumaker writes:

> This California self is the ultimate expression of modern individualism in its most inward, narcissistic, self-centered, and self-serving form. To the California self, the primary reason for living is to make the right choices and to consume the right things in order to maximize pleasure and minimize pain and, in general, to get the most from life. Yet this identity structure operates at a distance from the stabilizing effect of the wider community. The California self succumbs easily to states of psychic disruption due to its lack of emotional commitment to the commons and an identity that places inordinate emphasis

on personal and product outcomes.[11]

The California Self beams out from the West, across America. Radio and TV waves send it across the world, where it is picked up in books, magazines, and movies. Over the coming decades it will be the dominant personality of the West.

WHY "YOUTH" NOW APPLIES TO ANYONE UNDER SIXTY-SIX YEARS OF AGE

For all the supposed generational differences of our culture, all ascribe to the California Self. The first youth generation, the baby boomers, have struggled with the concept of growing up and thus have simply spawned more generations like themselves. The Rolling Stones are still touring, jeans are still cool, rock is stuck in perpetual revivals, kids still take drugs, and sex still sells. Nothing has changed. Sure, superficial trends will come and go, but the framework of the California Self still stays dominant in the West. No generation has yet rebelled against it, perhaps because the baby boomers staged the first and last great generational rebellion.

> THE ROLLING STONES ARE STILL TOURING, JEANS ARE STILL COOL, ROCK IS STUCK IN PERPETUAL REVIVALS.

HOW CALIFORNIA CREATED AN APOCALYPSE OF INDIVIDUALISM

Nathaniel West ends his commentary on California in *The Day of the Locust* with a scene of a riot that occurs at a Hollywood premiere. The public, wishing to see the stars on the red carpet, go rogue, pushing and fighting like a herd of angry animals. Violence breaks out, men start sexually abusing women, insults are thrown, people are crushed. West overlays the scene with parallels to the book of Revelation, painting the scene as an apocalypse of individualism. It's literally every man and woman for themselves.

Paradoxically as people push, shove, and give in to their basest individual desires, it is individuality which is lost. Today we are witnessing a similar apocalypse of individualism, we often fail to see it, so caught up in the pushing crowd are we.

The view of the universe as a cold and empty place is a frightening one. The concept of a completely immanent world sends Jim Stark crazy in *Rebel without a Cause*; it definitely sends Jack Kerouac and his friends into a kind of madness; and no one can look at Munch's *The Scream* without feeling the insanity inherent in the work as it stands at the beginning of the maddening, secular century that was to come. Today we have entered such a madness. It is mostly unnamed, but its effects are palpable.

To live with a truly immanent worldview is a horrible prospect, an existential nightmare of which the only solution seems to be suicide. Yet most who wander the pavements of the West do not seem driven to despair, although there is an undercurrent of depression, and suicide rates are high in developed and comfortable economies. But we in the West have intuitively created devises and distractions that stop us from asking the big questions about our worldview and all of its implications.

TEN:
SUPERFLAT

Visually stimulating but spiritually shallow. . .

HOW SECULARISM TURNED US INTO SUPERFICIAL BORES

Social commentator Hugh Mackay tells of attending a dinner party, where he found himself "seated beside a charming, articulate, professional woman who spent most of the evening telling me about her home renovations, including her new bathroom."[1] The big issues did not seem to grab her; the sweeping conversations that occurred in the past about life, religion, and politics were now replaced by the minutiae of home renovations. "It struck me that our endless quest for the perfect bathroom tile might have become a way of distracting ourselves from some other, larger question,"[2] Mackay observes. Like forms of sea life that are able to live in the pools left by low tide, we exist now in a shallow world. One in which the classic existential questions that have dogged humans for centuries are unknown.

> "IT STRUCK ME THAT OUR ENDLESS QUEST FOR THE PERFECT BATHROOM TILE MIGHT HAVE BECOME A WAY OF DISTRACTING OURSELVES FROM SOME OTHER, LARGER QUESTION."

When I was ministering in a downtown church, a number of Japanese backpackers started attending our services, asking me all kinds of questions about Christianity in broken English. I began to notice a pattern in their spiritual questioning, a common theme in their existential dilemma. They had grown up in the Japanese postwar economic miracle; they lived in mega-cities, which provided them with a kind of constant sensory overload. The artist Takashi Murakami has labeled Japanese contemporary culture Superflat,[3] because it lacks any kind of depth. It's visually stimulating but spiritually shallow. *Superflat* is an immanent worldview with a saccharine coating. Murakami links this retreat into the superficial to the atomic attacks that Japan suffered at the end of World War II.

Japanese young people are presented with an abundance of consumer choices and technological advancements but they are experiencing what Murakami calls "empty happiness," a sort of cute, cuddly, and naive hell.

JAPANESE KIDS GO ON THE ROAD

After high school or university these Japanese young adults would decide to go on an adventure. They would come to Australia to go on the road. They would rent a car and drive out into the utter desolation of the Australian outback desert, where one can drive for days and see nothing and be deprived of stimulation. Outside of their immanent, superflat world, these young people would have a spiritual and existential breakdown. By the time they arrived on our church's doorstep, the superflat distraction was detoxed out of their system and the big questions of life, God, human existence, and death were now at the forefront of their mind. Interestingly, when I later spoke at a Christian conference in Tokyo, virtually all of the Japanese

young people I met had come to faith while working or studying overseas. It was as if the superflat culture of Japan disabled
their ability to question reality with any depth.

Obviously superflat culture does not just exist in Japan.
Western culture has become just as superflat. Sure, we may not
have the garish cuteness of twenty-first-century Tokyo, but superflat is a kind of coping mechanism that has grown up in the
face of the immanent worldview. In the superflat response, the
horror and meaninglessness of secularism is simply ignored,
and a wall of distractions set up. When life starts to hurt, when
existential questions rear their heads, we just head out on the
road. Our sense of worry is lulled by the sound of our car moving through the night.

WHY NOTHING IS SACRED ANYMORE

Secularism is not just a rejection of the religious; it is also a rejection of the sacred. It is a desacralized world, in which no one or
no thing has any worth. Everything is disposable. Everything is a
commodity to be exploited. In such a world human relationships
are simply tools for the individual to use to find self-fulfillment. In
On the Road, when Sal and Dean reach San Francisco on one of
their trips westward, Dean forgets about their friendship, dumps
Sal, as well as Marylou, the girl he brought along on their cross-
continental jaunt, to go and be with Camille. Marylou, who has
literally been kicked to the curb, says that Dean will "leave you
out in the cold anytime it's in his interest."[4] Sal, who now has no
money and nowhere to stay and is thousands of miles from home,
agrees and looks wistfully back East. The immanent, desacralized
America may be great for "kicks," but it is a world where people
get used, and then thrown away.

HOW SECULARISM OBJECTIFIES WOMEN

For all of the talk of the transcendent nature of sex in *On the Road*, there is meaninglessness to it all. Sex is just another commodity to be consumed and discarded. Dean, Sal, and their male buddies sleep their way through the book, but the girls get left behind with the children and the responsibility. In one scene the girls confront Dean and his attitude toward women: "Dean, why do you act so foolish? . . . Don't you realize that you have a daughter?"[5] says Galatea. Dean grins awkwardly as the women close in on him and his irresponsible behavior. The pain Dean causes the women in his life seems to not worry Sal, who is bummed because he wants to go out and hit the clubs. Dean as a proto–Person of the Road is showing the lack of regard for relationship and commitment that will come to define the coming decades. Galatea continues her prosecution, "It never occurs to you that life is serious and there are people trying to make something decent out of it instead of just goofing around all the time."[6] Galatea is now getting to the core. Dean is the great irresponsible hipster hero to whom nothing is serious.

> THE UNIVERSE IS NOT A MEANINGLESS PLACE, THINGS DO MATTER, ACTIONS DO CATCH UP WITH YOU.

Back East, Carlo had questioned Dean and Sal regarding the motivation behind their road trips. Now on the West Coast, Galatea again poses the same question. "Now you're going East with Sal . . . and what do you think you're going to accomplish by that? Camille has to stay home and mind the baby now you're gone—how can she keep her job?" Silence again reigns as responsibility and consequence come crashing into the man-boy's immanent, adolescent fantasy world. Galatea and the girls expose one of the great myths of the immanent worldview. The universe is not a meaningless place, things do matter, actions do catch up with you. Sal, now deflated, describes the confrontation as "the saddest night . . . a pitiful dream."[7] Again Sal and Dean act as pioneer men of the road, a kind of male that will come to dominate the coming decades, a male who sees and uses women as objects, who runs from responsibility. The casual disregard that Dean shows toward the women in his life is a portent of the way in which women and increasingly men will be objectified in the twenty-first century. Dean walks ahead of the worlds of marital breakdown, the universes of porn, and the cosmoses of celebrity culture that are to come.

HOW WE BECAME OBSESSED WITH STUFF

It is telling that as Sal watches Galatea's dressing down of Dean, he wishes to escape and indulge his love of jazz. Sal is more worried about his musical obsession than about the human hearts that are breaking in front of him. In a superflat culture where nothing matters, we escape into obsessions and hobbies, interests that bear little ultimate consequence. In a commodified culture, we move and shift around meaning, giving weight to things that do not deserve mountains of time and attention. The twenty-first century will be a century marked by conspicuous consumption but also a flagrant misuse of time.

With religion off the agenda, our culture finds new avenues of devotion and distraction. Instead of moving us toward relationship and people, the immanent, superflat culture pushes us toward things. Millions of hours in the twenty-first century will be spent working through DVD TV series, scanning social network sites, gorging on celebrity gossip, downloading music, flipping through home magazines, and playing computer games. Things will take precedence over people. Meaningless activities will overtake our lives. There is nothing wrong with interests and hobbies in their right place, but the twenty-first-century culture will gorge on such activities. The real issues of human existence that have sat front and center of human consciousness have in the super-flat, immanent world been shoved aside. They are too heavy to be carried on the road. Instead we buzz across the surface of life, never venturing below the surface.

THE CULTURE OF WOOSH

Philosophers Hubert Dreyfus and Sean Dorrance Kelly under-stand that the immanent, secularized culture provides no greater sense of meaning. In lieu of a greater story, Dreyfus and Kelly insist that we look for "woosh" moments, those times when our favorite team scores a goal, the apex of the concert, the perfect meal. Rightly, they see the immanent world as something which pushes us toward individualism. They add that the best "woosh moments" occur when we are in the presence of others, especially experiencing them in a crowd. Dreyfus and Kelly call for us to experience moments of transcendence with a sense of gratitude, but to have the courage to not link them into a coherent narra-tive. They are careful to add that their theory of "wooshing up" "is nothing like the monotheistic, unified kind of certainty that the Judeo-Christian religions offer."[8] Rather, "wooshing up" has no greater purpose beyond simply this life.

Tellingly, to give their argument weight, Dreyfus and Kelly reach back into the ancient world, plumbing Greek thought. You cannot but help feel that Dreyfus and Kelly are trying to write a philosophy or a justification for those who want the personal autonomy that the immanent world brings, but with just enough touches and tastes of transcendent moments to keep us going. Without being attached to deeper reservoirs of meaning, what, really, are "wooshing moments"? Abraham Heschel wrote much about transcendent moments of awe, and of our experiences of the sublime in everyday life. For Heschel such experiences were "a way in which things react to the presence of God. It is never an ultimate aspect of reality, a quality meaningful in itself. It stands for something greater; it stands in relation to something beyond itself that the eye can never see."[9]

But for Dreyfus and Kelly there is nothing transformative about such experiences. They are simply there for momentary enjoyment, to be consumed like a chocolate which gives only a few moments of bliss. They don't offer the secular person anything apart from a fleeting distraction from our existential loneliness. The individual then finds themselves like an addict, with no hope of respite from their addiction, searching for the next "wooshing hit," something like Sal and Dean, constantly dissatisfied and on the road in the search kicks. If Heschel was right, all that "woosh" moments will do is make even more apparent our disconnection from a greater sense of meaning.

Although they are trying to find a way out of the deadening effects of secular living, by disconnecting transcendent moments of awe from any greater meaning or authority, Dreyfus and Kelly fail to see that "wooshing" moments are then ripe to be used as tools of manipulation. In a review of their work, David Brooks cautiously notes, "Though they try, Dreyfus and Kelly don't give us a satisfying basis upon which to distinguish the whooshing some people felt at civil rights rallies from the whooshing others felt at Nazi rallies."[10] You can see how the "woosh" idea has created "event" TV: without binding, meaningful cultural narratives, we now gather around the TV or hover over our web browsers to watch the final episode of *American Idol* or the launch of the latest gadget from Apple.

ELEVEN:

FEELINGS vs. FAITH

If I am not feeling good all the time,
something must be wrong...

O n the Road made such a splash upon its publication not just because of its frank depictions of sex and drug use, but because of the voice, then new and shocking. Sal talks in a confessional tone full of emotional language. Kerouac was trying to capture a new, authentic way of writing, one that captured the vitality and spontaneity of jazz. For the contemporary reader, this style of writing is familiar: we are used to confession, from reality TV to blogs to bestsellers. To us there is nothing strange about our inner worlds being spilled out into the public realm for all to see; yet for Kerouac's audience this was all radically new.

HOW WE ALL ENDED UP REVEALING TOO MUCH INFORMATION ON FACEBOOK

Richard Sennett in his book *The Fall of Public Man* powerfully illustrates how our private worlds have spilled over into the public realm. Traditionally, he notes, Western culture functioned accord-ing to a system of rules and etiquette that governed how we were to interact with one another in the public realm. It was impolite to talk too much about oneself; instead it was expected that the respectful person would be a good listener, inquiring into others' well-being before pushing one's own conversational agenda. Our modern age looks back at this form of social interaction as stuffy and repressed, excluding those who did not know the rules. Sennett counters by reminding us that such a system ensured social cohesion. Politeness and etiquette protected people from each other's dysfunctions and selfish behavior.

IF THIS WORLD IS ALL THERE IS, WHY WAIT PRACTICING HUMILITY AND PATIENCE WHILE YOUR FRIEND TELLS YOU ABOUT THEIR DAY?

This system of behavior was rooted in Christian values held by Western culture. Because individuals were created in the image of God and thus, good graces, politeness should be practiced as a form of social hospitality, one which gave dignity to the other. It also recognized that humans could be broken, dysfunctional, and sinful. However, the rise of secularism changed everything. Sennett notes that with the rise of the immanent doctrine and the belief in the immediate, the old social system is rejected. Character and integrity are out, personality and charisma are in. If this world is all there is, why wait practicing humility and patience while your friend tells you about their day? Spiritual development becomes passé; emotions, which are obvious and immediate, come to dominate all forms of public life.

HOW FEELINGS CAME TO SUBVERT FAITH

Sigmund Freud dismissed the Jewish faith of his youth and wrote off God as a longing for a father figure and an example of wish-fulfillment. Freud found his nineteenth-century Vienna office full of society women who had seemingly been driven to the hip social illness of the day—hysteria. A disciple of the immanent,

Freud placed the blame squarely on the social system with all its transcendent Judeo-Christian roots, labeling it repressive. According to Freud, the rich women in his office were ill and unhappy because polite society was keeping them from achieving their desires for sex, intimacy, and emotional gratification. For Freud, the whole of civilization was built upon repression. The more polite and respectful we are, the more we set up limits and behavioral taboos, the more hysteria and neuroses we suffer.[1]

> **THERAPY WOULD BECOME A SECULAR FORM OF SPIRITUAL DIRECTION AND THE THERAPIST WOULD TAKE ON THE ROLE OF THE NEW PRIEST.**

Thus the polite society began to crumble. Freud's ideas, initially scorned, began to take hold in the twentieth century. Limits and restrictions were out. Gratification was in. The baby boomers were to emerge postwar as the first generation for which self-denial and moderation were not lauded attributes but rather secular sins. Therapy would become a secular form of spiritual direction and the therapist would take on the role of the new priest. Therapy sessions would be the new confessional booths.

HOW THE THERAPEUTIC CULTURE DISTANCES US FROM GOD

In the therapeutic culture, our disconnection from God and the disillusionment that comes with cosmic meaninglessness is recast. We are told that we are not lost, not in need of eternal purpose. Instead we are told that our problems stem from our being out of touch with our feelings, or that we are stressed, sexually unfulfilled, or suffering a lack of intimacy. Therapy is an attempt to offer immanent cures for transcendent longings. Craig M. Gay writes that vast amounts of people now take "a therapeutic approach to . . . the problems of ultimate meaning and purpose, in short, to life itself and to life's most basic existential questions."[2]

Gay observes that therapy cannot provide "serious discipline for the soul" but only "the subjective experience of well-being."[3] The transcendent impulse toward spiritual perfection is replaced by an immanent goal of feeling good. A desire for well-being replaces the desire for salvation. Instead of facts we seek feelings; instead of objective truth we seek subjective sensations. Emotions win.

Everything is then judged by how it makes us feel. Today's blockbusters are now 3D sensory overloads; story lines are abandoned. Today's cinema, whether delivered in the home or at the movie house, is moving closer and closer to Aldous Huxley's vision of the "feelies" in his dystopian novel *Brave New World*. Our culture is becoming a "feelie" world in which something is only true and real if I can palpably feel it. If I am not feeling good all the time, something must be wrong. I judge my career, my marriage, and my faith by whether it makes me feel good. Truth is reduced into that which makes me feel good. Thus we prefer a form of faith that does not ask us to encounter our pain, to deny ourselves, to grow in areas which may be uncomfortable.

HOW BEING AUTHENTIC BECAME MORE IMPORTANT THAN BEING SPIRITUAL

Kerouac had little time for therapists and psychiatrists and lambasted his friends for using them. Yet filled with religious impulses and desires for the transcendent, he found himself seeking meaning in momentary touches of well-being. In Neal Cassady, Kerouac had discovered what he saw as an authentic man. Cassady (and his alter ego Dean Moriarty) conducted multiple affairs simultaneously, drank like a fish, and took drugs like others take hot dinners. Completely uninhibited, Cassady was emblematic of the contemporary authentic person, someone who in the parlance of therapy is honest about what he wants, "real" with himself. Today, honesty and authenticity no longer mean truthfulness, but rather a transparency concerning one's deepest wants and desires and an openness about one's determination to indulge in them.

We as a culture worship open, emotional communication. We are used to the politician breaking down when he is are caught out having an affair; we have seen a thousand Hollywood stars ecstatically babbling when they win an award. We expect to see directly the emotions of the victims of a natural disaster. We view such speech as authentic because it is communicated with feeling. Richard Sennett notes that today we mistake emotional nakedness and disclosure for community:

"IF EVERYONE IS JUST HONEST AND OPEN ABOUT THEIR FEELINGS WITH EACH OTHER, THEN EVERYTHING WILL BE ALL RIGHT" GOES THE MYTH.

> The reigning belief today is that closeness between persons is a moral good. The reigning aspiration today is to develop. . . experiences of closeness and warmth with others. The reigning myth today is that the evils of society can all be understood as evils of impersonality, alienation and coldness.[4]

This is classic therapeutic thinking: "If everyone is just honest and open about their feelings with each other, then everything will be all right" goes the myth. If the disclosing honesty of the therapist-client relationship can be experienced by everyone, the world will be OK. This is the elevation of interpersonal intimacy as the ultimate social goal. It is yet another way in which a person of the road seeks to find transcendence within the immanent world. Sennett claims that this hunger for intimacy is a direct result of the dislocation wrought by secularism: "Because of this dislocation, people sought to find personal meanings in impersonal situations, in objects, and in the objective conditions of society itself. They could not find these meanings. . . .They therefore sought to flee, and find it in the private realms of life."[5]

Thus the world of relationships, of sex, friendship, family, and marriage must now provide the solace and transcendence that God and religion did in the past. Sennett writes, "When the relations cannot bear these burdens, we conclude there is something wrong with the relationship, rather than with the unspoken expectations."[6] This is one of the factors behind the contemporary high divorce rate. A spouse must be an intimate best friend, provide the emotional support of a therapist, and be a supplier of constant sexual fulfillment. They also must possess the economic security of a banker, and the moral guidance of a pastor, while allowing enough relational distance so as not to impinge on their lover's personal autonomy.

The therapeutic culture has taught us to expect that relationships are one way. The relationship with the therapist is always one way, never mutual. The person receiving therapy expects to have their emotional needs met, to talk and to be listened to. The therapist's role is simply to facilitate the emotional well-being of the client. This expectation has left the therapist's office and now sets the tone for the relational world of the West.

WOULD THE REAL KEROUAC PLEASE STAND UP?

As you read Kerouac's journals and personal letters, you find a man very different from the hobo hipster portrayed in his books. The On the Road Kerouac we find mediated through Sal Paradise is always moving, always partying, always in the company of the strange, intriguing, and mysterious. He represents the romantic American ideal of freedom. Like the cowboy hero, he heads off into the yonder for more adventures at the close of the film. The real Kerouac we meet in his journals is much more ordinary. His time on the road comprises a few short trips during his twenties.

His real life is tremendously mundane. He lives with his mother and plays with his cat. Watches TV, goes shopping, and generally tries to make ends meet.

While he attends his fair share of Manhattan Beat parties, partying with the best of them, we also have the sobering image of Kerouac catching the train back to his mother out to the suburbs to make her breakfast. The romantic Kerouac is an intellectual with a liberal attitude toward sex and drugs and an artist's heart, able to quote Renaissance poets and match it with the best of the New York scene. Then, however, we have the small-town, working-class Kerouac, staunchly Catholic and politically conservative. Who loves baseball and home cooking. Who feels at home in a blue-collar bar, having a beer with ordinary working folks. The Kerouac who just wants to settle down with a simple woman, in a simple town. Thus we find Kerouac flying back and forth from these different personas in the same way he flies back and forth from the coast. Does he want to be romantic Kerouac or practical Kerouac? The answer is that he wants to be both. Again Kerouac is trailblazer for the lifestyles that are to come. Kerouac's confusion is rooted in two competing models, both offering ways to live within the immanent frame.

WHY THE BORING STUFF IN LIFE IS IMPORTANT

As we have established, the immanent world is the world of the practical. With a religious vision off the agenda, the worlds of finance, education, and work come to the fore. There is no hope in the eternal, the kingdom of God will not break out on earth, so we better get to work creating an immanent version while we can, one that does not require God's hand. Instead the secular version of shalom will be delivered by good organization, effective government, sound economic policy, and effective medicine and scientific advancement.

The citizen of an immanent culture must play their part by doing their duties. They must punch the clock, be a good worker. They must not indulge in antisocial behavior which could threaten the secular well-being of the collective. They must day after day bear the responsibility for playing their small but vital part of being a cog in the wheel of the secular machine. The secular citizen knows that if they play by these rules, pay their taxes and bills, food will always be on the table, they will have a secure place to live, social cohesion will continue, and they will be provided with the assurance of economic comfort. This was essentially the vision of mainstream Western culture during Kerouac's time and has been so for the last four hundred years—that is, except for a dissenting minority.

WHY EVERYBODY WANTS TO BE A NONCONFORMIST THESE DAYS

While the practical approach has delivered the West stable democracies with high standards of living, it has failed to deliver a sense of meaning. The problem with being part of the social, economic machine is that our individuality can be lost. The practical approach requires us to be cold, calculating, and logical, but humans are emotive; we feel strongly. The practical approach delivers us security and comfort, but it is a devil's bargain. We are forced to give up meaning and purpose in return. The middle-level manager of an accounting firm wakes at three in the morning and suffers a panic attack. What is he doing with his life? Where is this all going? Is it just this and then death? How can he go and sit in his open-plan office cubicle and do it all again tomorrow?

A stream of thinking began to emerge in the nineteenth century which was a critique of the practical approach yet was also shaped by its limits. Dissident voices suggested that the human was being lost in the machine. A diverse movement known as Romanticism sprang up. The Romanticist's task was a difficult one. Not wanting to return to the immanence provided by orthodox Christianity, the movement had to look for alternative sources of transcendence to Christian revelation and scripture. If the practical society demands that the individual be cold, calculating, and logical, then the romanticist should be warm, emotive, and illogical. Instead of work and toil, the romanticist will pursue art, creativity, and play.

If the practical society demands social conformity, the romanticists will be individualists and nonconformists. If industrial cities are springing up, the romanticist will look to nature for revelation. If the culture demands responsible living and conservatism, the romanticist will live with open abandon. If the practical society valued the technological advances of the West, the romanticist will look to the exotic, the foreign, and the tribal. If the practical approach encourages us to look outward to society, the romanticist will rebel by looking inward.

Yet to be a real romanticist you paid a price for your views. If practical culture valued security and comfort, the romanticist was to value suffering and discomfort. The ultimate mark of hip for the early romanticists was to nobly die an obscure death by consumption in a cold Parisian room, surrounded by amazing poetry that no one will read or ever appreciate. Not exactly what we want today.

Kerouac wanted to suffer and indeed he did. Yet after his sleepless nights on the road, after taking too many drugs and running out of money, there was always a warm bed waiting for him at his mother's house. Kerouac admitted that if it wasn't for his mother and her free rent offer, he would have never gotten any of his books finished.

We are a lot like Kerouac. The middle manager of the accountancy firm takes two weeks off from his job to backpack around Thailand, then returns home to the normalcy and routine of his job as he needs to pay the credit card debt he accrued on his journey. Then the gnawing for meaning kicks in again, so he starts a yoga class—which offers him a sense of physical well-being for a while but does not scratch the existential itch that the practical society exacerbates. What next? A thousand options lie before him. Take a poetry class, become a surfer, join a gym, have an affair, plant a vegetable garden, spend a year in Italy. Charles Taylor labels this phenomenon "the cross pressures," in which the whole culture "experiences cross pressures between the draw of narratives of closed immanence on one side, and the sense of their inadequacy on the other."[7] The person of the road then attempts to synthesize the two opposing approaches into one lifestyle. It was the baby boomers who first attempted this synthesis.

> **WE WANT THE STABILITY AND SECURITY OF HOME, YET WE FEEL THE ALLURE OF TRAVEL AND MOVEMENT.**

The tension between wanting a life of security and comfort and a life of meaning is felt clearly by most of us. The incredible Nietzschean burden of shaping lives of meaning in the face of a million consumer and cultural choices faces us all. We all expect products, experiences, and people to offer us transcendence. We want jobs that give us ultimate meaning, yet we want high pay packets. We want the stability and security of home, yet we feel the allure of travel and movement. We want unconditional love from family but the freedom to chart our own path.

TWELVE:

THE SLAVERY OF ABSOLUTE FREEDOM

Sin is denying yourself your desires...

French marketing guru Clotaire Rapaille was employed by Chrysler to sell Wrangler Jeeps to the American market.[1] After exhaustive interviews, Rapaille discovered that consumers wanted a vehicle that reflected their desire for freedom. They told stories of the open plains, of wanting to break free of the constraints of home, of wanting to connect with the American mythology of the Wild West. Rapaille created a campaign that reflected Americans' desire for a vehicle that delivered them that sense of freedom. A highly sucessful TV advertisement was crafted in which a Jeep was cast as a kind of modern-day horse, rescuing a small boy's dog, and then heads off into the sunset like a cowboy hero at the end of the movie. An iconic image, representing consumers' desire for mobility and freedom.

HOW OUR CULTURE OF FREEDOM STOLE OUR FREEDOM

This desire for freedom and autonomy is deeply intertwined with the worldview of the road. In her book *The Road Story and the*

Rebel,[2] film critic Katie Mills notes that the symbol of the road represents a new understanding of self, in which the individual attempts to break free from social relations, which lauds the value of personal freedom over everything else. This belief is seen everywhere today, especially in our low-commitment culture, where social commitments are now fluid and non-binding depending on the wants and desires of the individual. In the worldview of home, appointments and commitments were to be kept for the sake of the collective. In the worldview of the road, the individual's sense of autonomy and freedom rules over social cohesion. Yet freedom sometimes binds. Reflecting on freedom, psychologist Barry Schwartz cautions, "We should ask ourselves whether it nourishes us or deprives us . . . whether it enhances self-respect or diminishes it, and whether it enables us to participate in our communities or prevents us from doing so."[3]

Philosopher Isaiah Berlin[4] noted a number of years ago that there are positive and negative elements of freedom. There is a world of difference between the political prisoner sitting in jail because of his beliefs and the contemporary Westerner running from commitment, trying to maximize the opportunities to exercise his will. In a culture that offers no greater narrative than the road, unlimited freedom and choice can be terrifying.

HOW OUR IDEA OF COMMITMENT ENDED UP IN THE TOILET

Jonathan Franzen's novel *Freedom*[5] explores this kind of terrifying twenty-first-century freedom. *Freedom* tells the story of the Berglunds, an educated, liberal family drowning in a sea of freedoms. Characters in the book struggle with the freedom of a culture that allows them to "have it both ways." Franzen mirrors back to us the way that our culture's enshrinement of personal freedom creates a double mindedness. Throughout the novel, the key characters are caught in love triangles, moving backward and forward between potential lovers. Confusion and choice anxiety reigns. Franzen illuminates the way in which our opulent twenty-first-century freedom, unattached to any external moral order, results in a kind of moving paralysis, a fear to stand on either side of the line.

Like Kerouac, traveling backward and forward across America, Franzen's characters never find resolution, or home. One character, Joey Berglund, reflects that contemporary selfhood can feel like being "a collection of contradictory potential someones."[6] Unlimited freedom means that identity is fluid. The search to find oneself never ends.

In a survey of several decades of Western films, psychologist Jean Twenge notes that "the overall message of all of these movies . . . is to rebel against restrictive social mores. Don't follow the rules; do whatever makes you happy."[7]

IN THE CONTEMPORARY CULTURE THE MESSAGE IS CLEAR: HAPPINESS AND FULFILLMENT ARE FOUND IN BREAKING AWAY FROM COMMUNITY, SOCIAL EXPECTATIONS, RULES, AND TRADITION.

Twenge makes the observation that in these films, those who follow the rules are often crusty, repressed, uptight and, most of all, unhappy. Yet those who "follow their heart" or "their dream" (code language for the individual's desires) are always fun, carefree rule breakers, individualists who are sexually free and who ultimately receive happiness. In the contemporary culture the message is clear: happiness and fulfillment are found in breaking away from community, social expectations, rules, and tradition. Thus the life script of the contemporary world is to gain as much individual freedom as possible to assert one's desires, and this is achieved through escaping from relational and social expectations. It is completely Freudian in nature.

In their landmark study into the changing nature of American life, *Habits of the Heart*, Robert Bellah and his team note that the goal of life for the contemporary person is "to be your own person in the sense that you have defined who you are, decided for yourself what you want out of life, free as much as possible from the demands of conformity to family, friends, or community. From this point of view, to be free psychologically is to succeed in separating oneself from the values imposed by one's past or by conformity to one's social milieu, so that one can discover what one really wants."[8]

Tradition and social expectations thus replace sin in the contemporary imagination. In the Christian worldview, on the other hand, the sin of selfishness and the desire to be our own god prevents us from living full lives in both the immediate and the eternal. The Christian imagination encouraged us to view our desires, particularly our physical desires, with suspicion. But in the contemporary imagination, we must not rid ourselves of sin; we must rid ourselves of that which prevents our realizations of our desires. Thus post Freud, sin is vaporized for the person of the road. Sin is denying yourself your desires.

THIRTEEN:
FAITH ON THE ROAD

"I'm a typical American. Half of me is dying to give myself away, and the other half is continually rebelling."
David Foster Wallace

Modern evangelical culture, author John Leland notes, sprouted out of Kerouac's revered Southern California. Kerouac's call for mid-century America to go on a spiritual journey was heeded by "born-again" Christians. Some of the postwar Californian baby boomers and others, following on the heels of Kerouac's example, would launch the contemporary church movement, a movement which, like Kerouac, rejected convention and embraced casual dress, the therapeutic over the rational, and experience over dogma. The contemporary Christian movement would use language almost lifted from *On the Road*, such as "walk," "spiritual journey," and "seeker." Kerouac's mystical, medieval, saintlike visions, experienced in the everyday grime of life, echo the experiential and sensory touches of the Spirit that Charismatic Christians would experience in the seventies and eighties. Leland wonders whether Kerouac's true legacy is Christian rock, the Vineyard denomination, and Rick Warren's goatee.

HOW KEROUAC CREATED
CONTEMPORARY CHRISTIAN CULTURE

Leland is certainly on to something. More than anything, Kerouac embodied the contradictory approach to faith that is so evident today amongst many believers—one moment fully Christian, the next acting as if God did not exist.

One of the great contradictions of Kerouac's life is his contradictory relationship to his faith. Kerouac knew his Bible; his journals are filled with references to God; he writes his own psalms as prayers to God; he sits in church weeping; he wears a cross around his neck to provoke and annoy intellectuals; he calls himself a traditional Catholic and desires a religious rebirth in America. Yet simultaneously, he sleeps his way across the country, drugs himself silly, treats women like disposable napkins, and exhibits a selfishness that at times defies belief. How do we process and understand his seemingly confused approach to faith? John Leland wryly observes that:

> Kerouac's Church of the Road, in fact, is uncommonly genial in its commandments. Premarital sex, drugs, divorce, prostitution, homosexuality . . . all fit neatly into its gospel. . . . This church demands no tithes . . . or service to others. . . . The only requirement is unblemished self-absorption.[1]

Kerouac crafts and creates his own Christian faith in a collage approach combining elements of traditional Catholicism, Zen Buddhism, contemporary hedonism, romanticism, mysticism, and individualism. It is not systematic; rather it is filled with tensions, inconsistencies, and cognitive dissonance. It is ramshackle, constructed on the road. It belies logic and defies theological cross-examination.

Kerouac's faith confuses those trying to put him into a box.

He is revered as a countercultural figure by the bohemians on the left who laud his hedonism and balk at his faith. He is rarely claimed by Christians who struggle with his less-than-holy behavior. He does not fit in the neat categories of believer and nonbeliever that we are used to. We are more comfortable with well-articulated statements of belief or non-belief. We like the articulate apologist of faith; we are used to the rational atheist who through a sequence of arguments defends his nonbelief. We are used to the committed believer who strives to live according to the beliefs and convictions that shape her life. We don't know what to make of Kerouac's half-faith. Yet Kerouac's half-faith is the faith of so many today. Again we find him to be ahead of his time.

> **WE DON'T KNOW WHAT TO MAKE OF KEROUAC'S HALF-FAITH. YET KEROUAC'S HALF-FAITH IS THE FAITH OF SO MANY TODAY.**

THE BAGGAGE CLAIM

I stand at the baggage claim. Again I am in an airport, again I am exhausted. I think about returning home to my family, my friends, and my ministry. It occurs to me that I have now been in ministry full time for seventeen years. As the bags pass by me, I think of all the countless young adults who have passed through my life during my years of ministry. I think to myself that I cannot do it anymore. I think of the hundreds if not thousands of coffees with young adults deconstructing their faiths, I think of the countless hours spent with people in discussions, conferences, events, and seminars dissecting the Church, dismembering Christian culture, hunting down the elusive ideal of relevance. I think of the masses of people I have been in Christian "community" with, people who enter your life for a time intensely, who share their darkest secrets and brightest hopes with you. People you pray with, cry with, worship with. Then after a few months, a year, or, if you are fortunate, a few years, they then pass out of your life. Later you bump into them at malls, parties, or downtown. There is that awkward moment, when you realize that the embers of faith have almost died out. Then comes the telltale line "I still believe in Jesus, but . . ." People who want to hold on to the certainty of faith but who wish to have the freedom of the secular, who end up crafting their own version of Christian faith. People who are happy to live on the fence between faith and disbelief. People who unwittingly end up using you because at the center of their new mode of faith is the selfishness of radical individuality. As the bags pass by me the way people come in and out of my life, my gut yearns for a different reality, the rediscovery of an older concept of faith, one rooted in faithfulness and devotion. Yet such ideals seem lost in our day.

HOW CHRISTIANS AND ATHEISTS GET IT WRONG

To the despair of both the committed Christian and the staunch atheist, the real story of faith in the West over the last seventy years is the emergence of a strange hybrid faith, a mutation, the grafting of secularism onto a Christian skeleton. Go into any large bookstore and you will see books like Tim Keller's *Reason for God* and Rick Warren's *The Purpose Driven Life* sitting on the shelf right next to Richard Dawkins' *The God Delusion* and Christopher Hitchens' *God Is Not Great*. These titles do not so much confront each other in opposition but rather reach out to the uncommitted masses in the middle who want it both ways, who want to believe that there is a deeper magic in the world, a benevolent deity and an afterlife, and yet who revel in the hedonistic freedom that a secular worldview brings. People who sense a deeper magic in the world, who yearn for a greater meaning than

> THE REAL STORY OF FAITH IN THE WEST OVER THE LAST SEVENTY YEARS IS THE EMERGENCE OF A STRANGE HYBRID FAITH.

just malls, mochas, and minivans, yet who resist going all the way
to the destination of faith, because it seems too hard, too weird,
or just too much work. People who remain on the road, in between
the destinations of faith and unbelief.

Such people do not know what to do when they experience
the transcendent; when they experience a religious moment, they
can only processit through the framework of secularism, pushing
it into the private. Martin Robinson in his book *The Faith of the
Unbeliever* writes:

> Just occasionally there seems to emerge the sense that there
> might be something more than the merely physical. It is almost
> as if the existential encounter with the world occasionally sug-
> gests a religious dimension, but a knowledge of how to express
> such feelings is absent. In any case, it is as if the emergence
> of such feelings must at all costs be denied and suppressed,
> kept so firmly within the realm of the private that such longings
> dare not be admitted even to those few people with whom one
> shares some intimacy—one's friends, one's lover, one's wife.[2]

They struggle to articulate their views to pollsters and researchers; their views change by the day, even by the hour. Their
views are an attempt to live a contradiction, a set of beliefs that
defy logic. Their approach to faith and life is one built not on an
intellectual set of beliefs; rather it is shaped by pragmatism. It is
a do-it-yourself ramshackle construction thrown together, light
enough to pick up and transport when consumer culture demands
that we change allegiances. It is the ideal moveable shelter for the
psychically homeless of the West. Perfect for enjoying the sunny
days of twenty-first-century hedonistic culture. It is, however,
a shanty that is most definitely not adequate shelter when life's
storms truly strike.

HOW KEROUAC AND FREUD MADE SOME SINS
COOL FOR CHRISTIANS

Kerouac, living at the dawn of the permissive society, models a kind of Christianity that values both faith and the transgression of moral codes, laying the foundation for today's young adult Christian culture. Christians always seem to be trying to analyze what has just passed, rather than what is currently occurring. Christian culture for the last twenty years has been obsessed with dismantling what is seen as its sometimes stifling moral code. However, the reality of today's young adult Christian culture is radically different. Brett McCracken, in his study of progressive young adult Christian culture, notes that today certain behaviors, once considered out of bounds for Christians, such as smoking, drunkenness, sexual activity, and consumption of highly violent or sexually explicit entertainment, are now not only acceptable but cool. McCracken recalls:

"I WONDERED THAT NIGHT, AND ESPECIALLY IN THE DAYS THAT FOLLOWED: WOULD A NON-CHRISTIAN WHO CAME TO THAT PARTY HAVE ANY CLUE THAT THESE REVELERS WERE PEOPLE DEVOTED TO FOLLOWING CHRIST?"

> I recently went to a party with a lot of Christian hipsters in Los Angeles. It was a fun party, and everyone seemed to be having a great time. But I wondered that night, and especially in the days that followed: would a non-Christian who came to that party have any clue that these revelers were people devoted to following Christ? After all, the party was full of alcohol, drunkenness, people doing shots, dancing to filthy music, smoking, cursing, and who knows what else. This behavior is hedonistic and "cool," yes. But is it Christian?[3]

Considering that contemporary Christian culture in the West exists within the larger, permissive culture, built upon the modernist value of transgression, the Christian who questions such behavior is labeled pharisaical, repressed, or fundamentalist. Yet the rise of such behavior reveals much about how young adult Christians understand their place in contemporary culture, exposing how we are disciples of Sigmund Freud. In his work *Civilization and Its Discontents*, Freud theorizes that our innermost, primal desires must remain in check if we are to live in a comfortable, peaceful society. Thus certain behaviors become ways of letting off steam: the man driving his car yells and honks at other drivers as a way of releasing the valve of the murderous anger and violence he subconsciously feels; the married woman's daily flirtations with the handsome young barista at Starbucks are a way of sublimating her inner desires to be with men other than her husband. Thus many contemporary Christians follow Freud's lead. The Christian engaged couple have premarital sex, telling themselves that what they are doing is better than their promiscuous secular friends. The young adult ministry leaders get together and drink too much, as a way of releasing the valve of having to be the responsible ones all the time. The young pastor with conservative, evangelical theology cusses in his sermon, enjoying the thrill that comes with feeling transgressive. Such behaviors are not so much about the line between acceptable and non-acceptable Christian behaviors, nor are they about becoming less pharisaical to be more missional. Instead they reveal to us the inner rage that this generation of young Christians feels at having to live out their faith in a permissive, hedonistic society. They show us how much we have fallen for the beliefs of the morally insignificant universe, and for Freud's vision of human life.

Freud gets it half right: we do act in certain ways to release valves. Yet the Christian story tells us that what lies beneath are not primal instincts, but primal sins. There is no such thing as valves, only actions pointing toward or away from God. Such behavior flows directly from a misunderstanding of God.

HOW JESUS BECAME DELIVERER
OF OUR WANTS AND WISHES

Christian Smith and Melinda Lundquist Denton's research into the spiritual and religious lives of American teens exposed to the public the way in which the faith of the road has spread throughout the West. Smith and Denton discovered that underneath the noses of religious leadership, a mutant faith has grown up. Teenagers across the religious spectrum, Christian, Jewish, Hindu, and Buddhist, articulated an approach to religion that Smith and Denton have labeled Moral Therapeutic Deism. Its tenets are:

1. A God exists who created and orders the world and watches over human life on earth.
2. God wants people to be good, nice, and fair to each other, as taught in the Bible and by most world religions.
3. The central goal of life is to be happy and to feel good about oneself.
4. God does not need to be particularly involved in one's life except when God is needed to resolve a problem.
5. Good people go to heaven.[4]

Smith and Denton note that the teenagers in their study would not explain Moral Therapeutic Deism as clearly as stated above; rather it was an approach to faith that was imbibed from media, parents, and peers. It contains a moral element—"being nice to others"—but a moral element that would struggle to deal with the more serious ethical challenges that life brings. Its moral element is naive at best, based on a desire for basic social cohesion and the desire of the individual to be thought of as "likable." At its core,

Moral Therapeutic Deism is not a product of a religious imagination but is an attempt to mold faith around the expectations and authority of the individual. The researchers note:

> Moral Therapeutic Deism is . . . about providing therapeutic benefits to its adherents. This is not a religion of repentance from sin, of keeping the Sabbath, of living as a servant of a sovereign divine, of steadfastly saying one's prayers, of faithfully observing high holy days, of building character through suffering, of basking in God's love and grace, of spending oneself in gratitude and love for the cause of social justice . . . Rather, what appears to be the actual dominant religion . . . is centrally about feeling good, happy, secure, at peace. It is about attaining subjective well-being.[5]

The countercultural elements of faith that challenge and offer correction to persons of the road are jettisoned. That which provides the individual with a sense of well-being is retained. Moral Therapeutic Deism shows us the way that faith has been retained but remixed to provide a sense of solace in a predominantly secular worldview. It does not offer a salvation of transcendence which guarantees eternal life, it does not offer redemption, the culmination of history with God ensconced in the New Jerusalem; instead it offers an individualistic, immanent transformation, our culture's vision of the good life delivered by Jesus in a UPS truck.

HOW WE BECAME AGNOSTIC CHRISTIANS

Religious historian Philip Jenkins notes that the way that the West has reshaped Christian faith is paralleled by the way that it has reshaped marriage.[6] De facto relationships and cohabitation are now commonplace in Western countries. This was not the case only a few decades ago. De facto relationships are essentially marriages minus the biblical value of covenant, reshaped by a consumerist worldview that lauds the autonomy of the individual. A similar reshaping has occurred with faith, or should we say de facto faith: relationship with God is retained, but the autonomy of the individual remains. Theologian Tom Frame uses the term Christian Agnosticism to explain the road approach to faith that owes "a debt to both Christianity for its basic forms and agnosticism for its lack of conviction."[7] Frame explains that Christian Agnosticism is able to "bring a little transcendence to what would otherwise appear morbid."[8] The individual is then able to stomach the immanent frame without resorting to a faith that demands commitment and complete adherence.

When faith is accepted, the options, and alternatives of contemporary culture do not disappear. The medieval world socially reinforced belief; in contrast the contemporary world undermines belief. The serpent's question to Eve, "What if . . ." echos around the secular world, providing the believer with a multitude of off-ramps along the highway of faith. Dreyfus and Kelly explain, "To say that we live in a secular age in the modern West is to say that even religious believers face existential questions about how to live a life."[9] Measuring life through the immanent worldview which demands instant gratification, many will happily accept faith as long as it promises to deliver the real-time results of well-being and if it provides pointers on how to maximize life in the immediate. If expectations are not met, many will continue on their way, searching out other options and opportunities that promise self-actualization.

HOW WE ALL BECAME CALIFORNIAN CHRISTIANS

In his classic work *East of Eden*, John Steinbeck notes that this bipolar approach to faith was foundational in California's culture: "The church and the whorehouse arrived in the Far West simultaneously. And each would have been horrified to think it was a different facet of the same thing."[10] This confusing approach to faith grew in the harshness of the Californian West. It was the perfect approach toward religion for the rugged individualists, the entrepreneurs, the cowboys, the snake-oil salesmen, and the gold rushers who inhabited the early West. God for the lonely, ascetic moments out in the desert, girls and vice for the return to town.

For years this approach to faith stayed within state lines. As European thought reached the crisis of atheistic despair, brought on by postwar existentialism, it was California that provided the solution to this impasse. Kerouac became a cult hero to the first real "youth" generations, giving the people of the road their saint, Dean Moriarty. Dean did not need a church, a community, a code of conduct. Dean set the rules. God turned up when it was convenient, to give the debauched madness a semblance of order and meaning.

Kerouac was seemingly telling the world that you *could* have it both ways. The freedom of the cowboy and the solace of God. The consolation of faith and the pleasures of the whorehouse. This belief, popularized by Kerouac, spilled out of California, out of Haight-Ashbury and across the world. Without it we could not have today's former Christian recording artists embracing their sexy new public personas by dancing like strippers in their music videos. We would not have the hedonistic, self-absorbed movie star thanking God as he receives his award for the R-rated movie he starred in, or people labeling themselves *Spiritual but Not Religious* on their Facebook profiles. Without it we would not have the spiritual and consumer marketplace that is the empire of Oprah; we would not have had Mohamed Atta, enjoying lap dances in his last days. We would not have millions across the world living their faith lives on the road. After all, as Dean says excitedly to Sal as they sped across the United States, "Everything is fine, God exists."[11] Dean is right when it comes to the existence of God. But was everything fine?

FOURTEEN:
THE ROAD TURNS INTO A NIGHTMARE

The moments of transcendence that Kerouac searched for in mid-century America seem quite humble. Many of them are connected to his experience of the American landscape, of mountains and plains. One of Kerouac's "wooshing" moments is described in *On the Road* as his alter ego Sal takes a ride on the crowded back of a truck driven by two Minnesota farm boys. The simple pleasure of the ride through the open countryside and the camaraderie of the fellow travelers hoboing their way across the United States created for Sal a transcendent moment. Kerouac sought to learn from the way that the poor and the marginalized enjoyed their lives. His expectations were low; he looked for simple pleasures in the midst of the everyday.

But again, this is where Kerouac is contradictory, falling short of his vision. He often sought non-ordinary experiences in an attempt to find a sense of transcendence, resorting to the use of narcotics to escape the ordinary.

WHY WE WANT TO SEE PEOPLE HUMILIATED ON TV

Our culture has little time for Kerouac's vision of finding transcendence amongst the mundane and the marginalized. Daniel Boorstin writes that "we expect a dramatic spectacular every week, a rare sensation every night."[1] The "woosh" moments that Dreyfus and Kelly refer to in the ancient world occur in the epics of Homer rather than everyday life. We may experience the "woosh" watching the star athlete stage the impossible comeback in the championship game, but what makes a transcendent "woosh" moment is the fact that it is a once-in-a-lifetime event. It is the rarity of the moment that creates its worth. Here is where we get caught in a bind: with no grand narrative offering us meaning, we desire constant "once in a lifetime" "woosh" experiences—which nature, and the mundane, have no way of offering us.

> **WE ARE SO USED TO PSEUDO-EVENTS THAT WE FAIL TO NOTICE THEM ANYMORE.**

Boorstin notes that the secular hunger for incredible experiences gave birth to an industry, built on delivering us "woosh" moments. Boorstin recounts that one of the issues that the early mass media faced was that there were not enough newsworthy events to fill newspapers. "We used to believe there were only so many 'events' in the world. If there were not many intriguing or startling occurrences, it was not the fault of the reporter. He could not be expected to report what did not exist."[2] Over time the media learned how to create the news, to craft what Boorstin labeled "pseudo-events."

We are so used to pseudo-events that we fail to notice them anymore. They are part of our mental landscape; they escalate our expectations of life, portraying life as a never-ending cavalcade of "woosh" moments. Networks offer us "Event TV," the Super Bowl halftime show, the *American Idol* finale, the MTV Music Awards. A pseudo-event makes us want an even bigger and better pseudo-event next time. Pseudo-events rely on shock, sex, color, imagery, sound, raw emotion, and novelty. They are non-rationalistic, loud, and experiential. Synthetic, manufactured attempts at transcendence, in which the individual becomes lost.

Contemporary public life then becomes a constant stream of pseudo-events. No longer are they found just in the realms of entertainment but also in politics and even religion. French social theorist and activist Guy Debord coined the term "The Society of the Spectacle" to describe our modern world, one in which the public constantly demand more spectacles to satiate their hunger for novelty and sensation. This is the age of the image in full flight, the natural habitat of the person of the road. A place in which sensation triumphs over reason. In *The Day of the Locust*, West describes the hunger for shock in his proto–Californian Selves, who have consumed all of the "wooshes" that the Golden State has to offer:

> Once there, they discover that sunshine isn't enough. They get tired of oranges, even of avocado pears and passion fruit. Nothing happens. They don't know what to do with their time. . . . They watch the waves come in at Venice . . . but after you've seen one wave, you've seen them all. The same is true of the airplanes at Glendale. If only a plane would crash once in a while so that they could watch the passengers being consumed in a "holocaust of flame," as the newspapers put it. But the planes never crash. Their boredom becomes more and more terrible.[3]

Ironically the more exposure to pseudo-events, the more "woosh" moments that you consume, the more you become bored and are thrown back into the mundane. This creates a terrible anger within the person of the road, West continues:

They realize that they've been tricked and burn with resentment. Every day of their lives they read the newspapers and went to the movies. Both fed them on . . . murder, sex crimes, explosions, wrecks, love nests, fires, miracles, revolutions, war. This daily diet made sophisticates of them. The sun is a joke. Oranges can't titillate their jaded palates. Nothing can ever be violent enough to make taut their slack minds and bodies. They have been cheated and betrayed.[4]

West's Californians hunger for the violent. In his book *Empire of Illusion*, Chris Hedges explores the way in which this violent hunger for pseudo-events and novelty is infecting American culture. Hedges cites reality television, which feeds upon humiliation and public shaming; professional wrestling as a cruel pantomime based on aggression and degradation; celebrity culture, which feeds off the personal tragedies and addictions of the well-known; and the porn industry, which is no longer about sex, but rather violence and the debasement of women. Hedges notes that underneath all of these pseudo-events there is a dark side to the "woosh" culture, a current of anger, a resentment against the "dream not coming true," about the ideal being crushed by reality.

HOW OUR CULTURE DISCONNECTS US
FROM EVERYDAY LIFE

Those who constantly seek pseudo-transcendence become disconnected from the real issues of the day. Global poverty, environmental disaster, war, and conflict, in the words of Hedges, "rarely impinge to prick the illusions that warp our consciousness. The words, images . . . and phrases used to describe the world in pseudo-events have no relation to what is happening around us."[5] Dreyfus and Kelly's idea that we find meaning through "woosh" moments might sound fantastic to those who have the financial clout for courtside seats during the playoffs, who inhabit the corporate boxes at the U2 concert, and who can afford to snorkel off the shore of the luxury resort. Yet what solace does it offer to the mentally ill stuck in the cycle of the streets? What hope does it offer to the refugee fleeing war? How does it aid those who wonder how they can feed their children in the morning? Thus the lifestyle of seeking the transitory moments of pseudo-transcendence is exposed for all of its shallowness and selfishness. Truth is the casualty of the age of the image. The hunt for "woosh" moments only leaves us mired in illusion. Hedges continues:

> Blind faith in illusions is our culture's secular version of being born again. These illusions assure us that happiness and success is our birthright . . . They promise that pain and suffering can always be overcome by tapping into our hidden, inner strengths. They encourage us to bow down before the cult of self.[6]

Therein lies the trap. We attempt to escape the mundane through seeking out transcendent experiences. Yet the essence of transcendence is rooted in "the other," the transcendent is mysterious because it is not known, it is otherly. The culture of illusions, peddling pseudo-transcendence, will always leave us unsatisfied because it does not lead to another, it simply leads back to ourselves. The age of the image prophesied by Boorstin leads us not into worship of another, but instead ourselves. John Ralston Saul writes:

> The Death of God combined with the perfection of the image has brought us to a whole new state of expectation. We are the image. We are the viewer and the viewed. There is no other distracting presence. . . . The electronic image is man as God and the ritual involved leads us not to a mysterious Holy Trinity but back to ourselves.[7]

We exist in an idolatrous society, one in which the ultimate idol is the self.

HOW THE ROAD SENDS US MAD

By the end of *On the Road*, Sal's opinion of Dean has dramatically changed. At a party, Dean arrives like a kid with attention-deficit disorder. He can barely string a coherent sentence together and moves around the party in a confusing buzz. The gang has now grown up; they are wedded to the responsibility that accompanies family and paid work. Yet the road has kept Dean in a suspended adolescent fantasy. Rather than maturing, he has regressed to an almost childlike figure. No longer do the guys look at him in awe, or the girls with desire. Now they only look at him with parental

DEAN HAS JUMPED THE SHARK. THE ROAD HAS SENT HIM MAD.

pity. Dean has jumped the shark. The road has sent him mad. No longer does Sal view Dean as a great cowboy hero who will take him away from the mundane nature of his East Coast life. He is now to be feared. Manic, self-obsessed, and without morals, he has succumbed to the idol of self. Sal now sees Dean as an angel of death:

> Suddenly I had a vision of Dean, a burning shuddering frightful Angel, palpitating toward me across the road, approaching like a cloud, with enormous speed . . . bearing down on me. I saw his huge face over the plains with the mad, bony purpose and the gleaming eyes; I saw his wings; I saw his old jalopy chariot with thousands of sparking flames shooting out from it; I saw the path it burned over the road; it even made its own road and went over the corn, through cities, destroying bridges, drying rivers. It came like a wrath to the West . . . Everything was up, the jig and all. Behind him charred ruins smoked. He rushed westward over the groaning and awful continent again, and soon he would arrive.[8]

Sal's dreams of a life of happiness and contentment with a simple girl in a simple home are now threatened by the specter of Dean. Dean has become the road. He is now a cautionary figure. A tragedy. Oversexed, narcissistic, and adolescent, he is the embodiment of the worst elements of the twenty-first-century self that is to come.

WHY WE PREFER WOW TO THE WORD

If there is one word that captures our culture's desire for the pseudo-transcendent it is the word "wow." One of Kerouac's intentions in writing *On the Road* was to create a new language, one that corresponded with the new experiential culture that was emerging. The term "wow" perfectly captures this new idea of living and speaking. It is a word that does not really mean anything, yet seems to suggest that something incredible has happened. It is not a measured response, nor a reflective description. Rather it is simply a visceral, therapeutic utterance. Its use indicates that an experience has been consumed. Literary critic Amy Hungerford notes the constant use of the word "wow" in *On the Road*.[9] It flows out of the mouth of Dean in a steady stream. After hanging out with Sal, Dean begins to adopt his language and use of the term. As he hitches a ride into Denver, eagerly anticipating reconnecting with his beat buddies, he re-imagines himself as a kind of religious prophet, one who brings a new gospel of wow:

> I would be strange and ragged and like the Prophet who has walked across the land to bring the dark Word, and the only Word I had was 'Wow!'[10]

Sal's friends whoop and yell and throw out wows, anticipating the hyper mood that will envelop life in the coming decades. Wow is the sound of now, it captures our world awash in noise, sound, and color. It is the mantra of the media madness in which we now swim. Yet in one poignant scene high up in the mountains over-looking Denver, as the speakers of the new language of "wow" whoop and scream into the night air, Kerouac reveals the need for another kind of word:

> We fumed and screamed in our mountain nook, mad drunken Americans in the mighty land. We were on the roof of America and all we could do was yell, I guess—across the night, east-ward over the Plains, where somewhere an old man with white hair was probably walking toward us with the Word, and would arrive any minute and make us silent.[11]

Kerouac waits for the word that will make him silent. The word that will arrest the constant search for kicks, that will rein in the hedonistic binge, that will end the ceaseless wandering on the road. We too wait with Kerouac for the word that will make us silent. The Word would come for Kerouac. Reaching him, when he had reached the end of America, and the end of himself.

FIFTEEN

AT THE END OF THE ROAD
A CROSS

"God will come into me like a golden light..."

If *On the Road* launched the "Rucksack Revolution," encouraging a whole generation to chase experience and self-absorption, Kerouac's *Big Sur* maps out the consequences of the life script he championed in his early years. Approaching forty, suffering from chronic alcoholism and running from the media and the movement he inspired, Kerouac retreats to his friend's shack at Big Sur in Northern California. Like the jumpers who take their own lives on Golden Gate Bridge facing the sea, he has exhausted the American continent in a search for meaning. There is no longer any land to consume, there is only the expanse of the Pacific, its void a reminder of his myth and his mortality. Kerouac reflects with horror that he is in the midst of a "physical and spiritual and metaphysical hopelessness you can't learn in school no matter how many books on existentialism or pessimism you read.[1] Kerouac is aging; the handsome young traveler of *On the Road* is well and truly gone. "The face of yourself you see in the mirror with its expression of unbearable anguish so haggard and awful with sorrow you can't even cry for a thing so ugly, so lost, no connection whatever with early perfection."[2] The open road is now at an end, youth is gone and no longer offers any potential. Instead he is only left with "the fear of eerie death."[3]

THE CRACK-UP AND THE CROSS

In the shack surrounded by cliffs and rock, Kerouac is visited by sheer terror. Years of drug use, alcohol abuse, and lostness result in a nervous breakdown. Sitting on the edge of America, he is pushed to the edge of insanity. In *On the Road*, Sal's aunt (the alter ego of Kerouac's own mother) warns of the dangers of the road. Years later her predictions had come true. In *Big Sur*, Kerouac writes, "Ma was right, it was all bound to drive me mad, now it's done—What'll I say to her?"[4] No longer free on the road, but now enclosed within the walls of the shack, Kerouac in desperation, losing his mind, writes, "I'm crying, I'm not human anymore and I'll never be safe anymore." Voices rush through his head, in languages that he cannot understand. Kerouac at his utter limit, in panic exclaims, "The devil!—the devil's come after me tonight! Tonight is the night!"[5] Then with a jolt a vision comes before Kerouac.

> I SEE THE CROSS, IT'S SILENT, IT STAYS A LONG TIME, MY HEART GOES OUT TO IT, MY WHOLE BODY FADES AWAY TO IT.

Having feasted on America, having consumed every drug, every last drink, every highway, fame, sexual experiences, the mysticism of the East, and the American dream, Kerouac writes, "Suddenly as clear as anything I ever saw in my life, I see the Cross." At the end of the road stands the Cross. Kerouac has in a sense returned home, to the truth of his youth. He is back kneeling before the Cross of his childhood: "I see the Cross, it's silent, it stays a long time, my heart goes out to it, my whole body fades away to it. I hold out my arms to be taken away to it." Kerouac, the broken hipster, the fallen literary star immersed in the reality of his sin, prays, "I'm with you, Jesus, for always." In shock Kerouac writes, "I lie there in a cold sweat wondering what's come over me for years my Buddhist studies and pipesmoking assured meditations on emptiness and all of a sudden the Cross is manifested to me—My eyes fill with tears."[6] The next day a different man emerges: "Blessed relief has come to me from just that minute. Everything has washed away—I'm perfectly normal again...I'm sitting smiling in the sun, the birds sing again, all is well again."[7] The journey is now over, Kerouac thinks not of the road, but of home:

> I'll get my ticket and say goodbye... and leave all San Francisco behind and go back across autumn America and it'll be like it was in the beginning.... My mother'll be waiting for me glad.... On soft Spring nights I'll stand in the yard under the stars—Something good will come out of all things yet—And it will be golden and eternal just like that—There's no need to say another word.[8]

Kerouac would return home to Lowell, where he would marry Stella Sampras, the sister of his childhood friend Sammy, who was killed during the war. Stella would love him unconditionally and with patience, nursing him through his addiction. Ben Giamo, biographer of Kerouac's spiritual journey, would write of Kerouac's final years, "Thus cleansed, Kerouac returns home in mind, body and spirit—to the 'blessed relief' of the Cross and all that it stands for.... His later years...show a far more unmitigated attachment to the sorrows and sacrifices of Jesus."[9] Giamo notes that Kerouac had now moved from trying to be a Buddhist "Bhikku" and was now a penitential sinner. He became fixated upon the Cross, turning his hand to painting and drawing countless images of Christ and His crucifixion.

THE END OF THE ROAD

Like Moses never reaching the Promised Land, Kerouac never fully reached the peace he sought in his life. His last years, while pointing to Christ, are still filled with the ravages of his earlier life choices. He is still wracked by addictions. In 1968 news reaches him of Neal Cassady's death. Unlike Kerouac who had walked away from the road, Cassady had continued seeking "kicks," fully embracing the hippie revolution and traveling across the United States in hippie author Ken Kesey's Technicolor bus. Cassady is found dead in a field after consuming an incredible amount of alcohol and drugs. The road had finally claimed him. A year later Kerouac would also be claimed, years of alcohol abuse causing his insides to revolt. One day sitting in front of the TV he would start vomiting blood. Kerouac had come to believe that he was called by God to suffer for his sins, to "moan for man," and suffering would mark his final hours on this planet. For fifteen hours, his insides hemorrhaging, he would writhe, screaming and spluttering out blood. A born fighter, Kerouac would tenaciously hold on to life.

A call for blood transfusions would see his wife Stella give blood, as well as a member of the American Nazi party, who a lonely Jack had spent time talking to in the weeks before his death. The saintly Stella, next to the Nazi, giving blood for Jack, seemed a fitting final epitaph to the two sides of Kerouac's life. While he was surrounded by his friends and family for most of his final hours, strangely all were absent the moment he passed into eternity. Perhaps fittingly for a life marked by a quest for solitude, Kerouac would die God's lonely man. Legendary CBS news anchor Walter Cronkite would announce on the evening news, "Jack Kerouac, the novelist who wrote *On the Road*, reached the end of it today."[10]

As the final arrangements for his funeral were made, Kerouac's body would be held in the Archambault funeral home across the road from a set of Christian carvings. The carvings represented the Stations of the Cross. As a child in the twenties, Kerouac and his late brother Gerard would walk together, praying before each station, absorbing their meanings. The arc of his life was now complete. Kerouac's road had wound through the towers of Manhattan, through the expanses of the plains, to the tops of mountains. It would kiss the sugary lips of American success, descend into the valley of debauchery, pause before the lidded, ambivalent eyes of the Buddha, hold hands with madness, and return home to the simple, once-forgotten truth of the Cross. Kerouac, predicting his eternal future, wrote in his sketchbook shortly before his death, "God will come into me like a golden light and make areas of washing gold above my eyes and penetrate my sleep with his Balm—Jesus, his Son, is my Heart Constantly."[11]

OUR WAKE FOR JACK

Before pragmatism causes us to rush off in a blur of busyness in search of the perfect programs, political platforms, ministry techniques, and church shapes that will solve the problems created by the culture of the road, we must sit, we must be still. We must bow our heads beside his body, and pause. We need to be quiet; we need to sit with Jack in wake, listening to the lessons of his life.

PART 2

SIXTEEN:
THE ROAD HOME

Life is not about moments of pleasure. It is about a naked, face-to-face encounter with God.

Copenhagen is as beautiful as its citizens. Walking around the city I could understand why so few people in Denmark attend church.

WHY DANISH PEOPLE DON'T NEED GOD

As I watched a family eat dinner on the yacht moored in the canal out the front of their beautiful eighteenth-century house, I asked myself, "Who would need God here?" Everywhere I turned were attractive, fashionable young people riding bikes in the summer sun. The whole city reflects the Danish design ideal; everything is simple, elegant, and chic. The Danes have a culture code which underpins so much of their culture. In Danish, the term is *hygge*, a word difficult to translate into English. Essentially the term captures an idea of coziness, a communal idea of peace and tranquility in which life is not interrupted by

> I ASKED MYSELF, "WHO WOULD NEED GOD HERE?" EVERYWHERE I TURNED WERE ATTRACTIVE, FASHIONABLE YOUNG PEOPLE RIDING BIKES IN THE SUMMER SUN.

distractions, negativity, or anything annoying. The city reflects this ideal. As I think of this desire for comfort I cannot but help think of Søren Kierkegaard, the great nineteenth-century, melancholic Christian philosopher. How did his radical Christian philosophy, so built around our loneliness and pain, come out of such a place?

I decided to visit his grave. As I enter the cemetery the sun breaks through the trees. All around me on the lush grass sit stylish, attractive Danish young people picnicking, making out, drinking wine and smoking cigarettes. It feels like I have stepped into a Scandinavian Ralph Lauren commercial. It was the epitome of *hygge*. Yet jutting up in between these groups of young adults were roughly hewn, weather-beaten, centuries-old graves. Each tombstone speaking of our mortality, silently telling the young people caught in the ephemeral pleasures that this will all pass. The scene was parabolic: beneath the youthful, glitzy, glamourous, hedonistic veneer of our culture, our imminent death and need for an eternal answer could not be hidden.

I came upon Kierkegaard's grave, which sits humbly as part of his family plot. Kierkegaard's radical view of Christian life taught us that each one of us must face the reality of our cosmic aloneness, of our mortality. Our efforts to craft a life of pleasure, or even a life of good works, would pale into insignificance in the face of the reality that each of us must face death and God. Kierkegaard reminded his culture, so obsessed with comfort and with crafting a life that is free of the negative and the annoying, that the essence of life is an encounter with our fragility and mortality, an encounter which leads to God. Kierkegaard stripped back the distractions, reminding us of what is truly important in life. Kierkegaard's analysis reminds us that the road ends, that life is not about the experiences, the diversions, and moments of pleasure. It is about a naked, face-to-face encounter with God.

THE ROAD VS. *ON THE ROAD*

If Kierkegaard was here today, I believe he would prefer Cormac McCarthy's Pulitzer Prize–winning novel *The Road* to Kerouac's *On the Road*. Whereas the road genre pioneered by Kerouac is an exploration of personal autonomy and future possibilities, *The Road* turns the genre on its head. It does not present us with an America of options and freedoms, it does not offer us a road to untold pleasures. Instead it presents us with a sick and dying world.

In *The Road* a global cataclysm has occurred. The earth and its creatures are dying. Most of the human population is dead. Those that have survived the horror have turned animalistic, reverting to blood cults and cannibalism. McCarthy paints the biblical story in reverse: the world is returning to a formless void. Sin and depravity abounds, children are sacrificed and humans have returned to the pagan worship of rocks. The spirit of Moloch has returned.

The central characters of the story are a father and son. They are never given names, they have very little backstory. The mother has taken her own life, unable to face the doom that is engulfing the planet. The father is also dying of an unnamed illness. His last desperate act of love is to travel across the dead landscape with his son to the sea, in the vague hope that something better will be there, something that will save the son.

The malls and stores are now looted, the cities deserted. The entire fabric of culture has unraveled. The father, unlike other road-genre protagonists, is not looking for personal freedom, pleasure, or excitement. Instead every fiber of his body strains to protect and keep his son alive. The tender and intimate conversations between father and son are in stark contrast to the cold dread around them. The book forces us to painfully examine our beliefs and values when they are distilled into the absolute essentials. We are forced to ask what really matters when the world is no longer there. The story tells us that when everything that is inconsequential is swept away, only love matters. The love that the father shows for his son is not therapeutic, nor romantic, it is self-sacrificing love at its most redemptive. The tender love of a father for his son is all that is left amongst the death and brutality. In a world which is soiled and stained, it shines like crystal, fragile and beautiful.

Throughout the book the term *secular* is used to describe the landscape. McCarthy also describes the world as Godless. Kerouac had set out on the road looking for moments of transcendence, for moments of natural revelation. The landscape spoke to him; it was a spiritual reprieve from the secularity of the city. Creation was his setting for self-discovery. Yet in the burnt landscape of *The Road*, nature is dying; it no longer speaks of God, of the transcendent. Rather it speaks of death and destruction. Evil seems to have won out against good. As the father and son make their way toward the coast, they find themselves trying to find God amongst the ruin, trying to make sense of the destruction of the world.

> AS THE FATHER AND SON MAKE THEIR WAY TOWARD THE COAST, THEY FIND THEMSELVES TRYING TO FIND GOD AMONGST THE RUIN, TRYING TO MAKE SENSE OF THE DESTRUCTION OF THE WORLD.

Finally the man and the boy reach the coast. The father has exhausted every last ounce of his energy in keeping his son alive, of getting him to a better place. Sadly there does not seem to be any respite from the cataclysm at the coast. The father dies in his son's arms. The boy sits with his father's body for three days, a deeply significant and symbolic number indicating *The Road*'s deep biblical subtext. On the third day a man appears. There is something different about him. He is not like the others that they have come upon on the road, those who have turned to cannibalism. The man asks the boy if he would like to come with him. The boy asks if the man has a little boy; the man tells him that he does. The boy asks if he eats children. The man says that he and his wife also have a girl, and that they do not eat children.

At the end of America, the road, and the world, redemption comes. The woman embraces her newly adopted son, and tells him about God, and that the breath of God is breathed into each man. At the end of everything, there is a family, there is love, there is God. These are the basic building blocks, the rudimentary elements of God's plan for the earth. McCarthy's telling of the story of the world in reverse ends with God. The woman telling the boy that the breath of God exists in each man echoes the image of God breathing life into Adam in the book of Genesis. Yet the book is not just about the past but also the future. The unnamed cataclysm seems human by design; it warns us of the possibility of a world flattened and destroyed by human hands. In the last paragraph of the book McCarthy writes, "Once there were brook trout in the streams,"[1] and that these fish "hummed of mystery." For the first time in the whole novel nature speaks, the world is again imagined alive. The image of the brook trout, deep in the waters, humming with mystery, is luminously transcendent in contrast to the deadness that has gone before. This morsel of transcendence is not found through hedonism, or through the quest for experience or autonomy. The transcendence and mystery only comes after a father's dying sacrificial love.

To rediscover a world of mystery and meaning we must return to that other road that leads back past Kerouac, past the sixties, past the culture of the road, the hippies, the teenagers, back past the effects of secularism. Back into the depths of time. Back to the symbol which contains the redemption of those who have followed the road. Back to the ultimate symbol of a father's love for his children.

THE CROSS

As we look out across the millennia, something grabs our attention. It seems small, weak, irrelevant. It is two wooden beams tied together. It sits two thousand years ago on a garbage dump. We almost did not see it: the light and noise pollution, the pumping soundtracks, the buzz, the tweets, and the twenty-four-hour news cycles almost took our attention away. Yet there it rudely sits. Before we know it, the noise, the heat, the distraction dies away. It rises up before us. The inane pop music is now gone, and all that remains is a steady beat, which we soon realize is our hearts pumping. Beneath our feet is dust, the dust from which we came, the dust that we will return to. Before we know it, all the lies of our culture, the spin thrown at the New Humans that youth lasts forever, that somehow the present moment will hang in the air for eternity, are exposed. Our cosmic smallness, our fragility, our mortality is brought into the blinding light. Standing here, our pathetic attempts to become mini-gods are revealed for the pitiful, cosmic charades they truly are.[2]

The cross is the apex of God's intervention in the world, a symbol which reminds us that God wishes to rebuild the world, to re-create us in His image. A very different road leads to this cross. It is not the smooth superhighway of the contemporary road, serviced with fast-food outlets. Instead it is a road worn through the desert by the march of individual feet. Millions of individual feet, called by God, each moving toward something bigger. A journey that began with a single step as Abraham was called out of the ancient city of Ur. The step that became a march as the people of God walked out of captivity in Egypt, as the prophets walked out of step with culture but in step with God. Footsteps wearing out a highway in the desert as kings and paupers chose God over idols, sacrifice over self, and justice over oppression.

Eventually this road, carved by so many feet, willed by God, would by joined by His feet. This road would not lead to a tantalizing possibility over a distant mountain, but instead would end with the sound of a hammer smashing bone, as God's feet would be nailed to a cross. Then the unthinkable would occur: God would die. Darkness would momentarily engulf the world. The universe would mournfully scream. Death, sin, brokenness, and horror would seemingly win. Yet somehow a price would be paid, a victory won. Out of the darkest moment light would flood, death would die, evil would be routed. God would be tortured and killed in your place.

Christ's body would be planted in the dead earth of a graveyard, just outside of Jerusalem. For three days it would lie in the cold ground, as dead and lifeless as the bricks of Babel. On the third day, God would explode out of the tomb, alive with a newness barely comprehensible. Mary, her cheeks moist with tears for her lost Rabbi, finds an empty grave and man whom she mistakes for a gardener. Only when she hears in her master's voice that tender intimacy, the call of her name, does she recognize the risen Christ. Christ's conversation with Mary reminds us of the precious, intimate language that McCarthy captures between the father and the son in *The Road*. The speech of a father who has given his life so that his child may live. To understand this triumph we must return to the road that led to this place. We must return to the first step of the road of devotion.

SEVENTEEN:
AN OLD KIND OF CHRISTIAN

The culture of the road has created a new generation
of passive young men...

Familiar with the rhythm of the road we struggle to comprehend that there is another way to be human. We are so used to being on the move, half-formed and half-committed, that we can barely imagine that an alternative exists. Only through understanding the way that our loving Father created us with a role and with a purpose can we rid ourselves of the worldview of the road. Yet those who should be closest to Christ, who should intimately understand His vision for our humanity, so often get it wrong. As the Church struggles to find its place in the culture of the road, we as individual believers, attuned to the constant self-reinvention of the road, wrestle with ever-changing meanings of what it is to be Christian in this time and place. We find all kinds of new labels, groupings, and subcultures sprouting up. Books and articles are churned out trying to keep pace with the birth of new movements. The Internet's ability to gather people of like mind in online ghettos has facilitated this fragmentation.

HOW WE FORGOT OUR GOD-GIVEN ROLE

For many, these tribes provide a sense of camaraderie, a place to gather with those who are committed to the same goals. These new groupings also provide a point of differentiation for the believer living in what some call a post-Christian culture, a way of distancing yourself from forms of Christianity that you would not want to be associated with. Sometimes, as with any tribes, war breaks out, yet today such battles occur on Facebook pages, blogs, and Twitter.

As I look across this new landscape, I can understand its allure. It feels good to sit in a conference surrounded by those of similar ilk, to walk into a room and know that you are on the same page with everyone, to speak in places where there will be agreement. Yet I feel as if our new movements and subcultures are not so much about belief but belonging. They tell us more about our search for meaning and identity in the culture of the road than they do about our theologies and practice.

> IT FEELS GOOD TO SIT IN A CONFERENCE SURROUNDED BY THOSE OF SIMILAR ILK, TO WALK INTO A ROOM AND KNOW THAT YOU ARE ON THE SAME PAGE WITH EVERYONE, TO SPEAK IN PLACES WHERE THERE WILL BE AGREEMENT. YET I FEEL AS IF OUR NEW MOVEMENTS AND SUBCULTURES ARE NOT SO MUCH ABOUT BELIEF BUT BELONGING.

New movements can become a way of welding an extra layer of identity to the Christian faith, because we feel that being Christian in and of itself does not offer enough. We become "_____ Christians." Our identity really is in the prefix. I know people who have already moved from one grouping to another, reinventing themselves, finding a new group of comrades, only to move on again when the road calls. I wonder if this is what God wants? I wonder why we take our lead from conferences, web pages, and books instead of looking to God Himself to understand our identities?

Jesus also lived in a world of religious factions

and contrasting identities. There were the liberal Sadducees who wished to fuse hip Greek thought with Judaism. There were the evangelical-like Pharisees who held to the Word of God, believing that holiness would redeem Israel. There were the countercultural Essenes, who refused to be part of the corruption of their culture, living off the grid in spiritual communes. Then there were the Zealots, who through a politics of force attempted to return Israel to her godly place. Scholars have tried to place Jesus in one of the competing camps. Yet such attempts are problematic, just as attempts to place Jesus in one of today's Christian factions seems an exercise in futility. Jesus' role and mission transcended the religious factionalism of His day. His purpose was cosmic in scope.

I am not suggesting that we leave our movements, or ditch our friends and comrades. Yet we must abandon the rules and regulations of the culture of the road to discover our true biblical purpose. We must look to Christ and His identity, not the meaningless movement of the road. Paul in 1 Corinthians would write, "'The first man Adam became a living being'"; the last Adam, a life-giving spirit."[1] Christ is the new Adam, yet whereas Adam failed in his mission, Christ will succeed. Adam was charged with a stewardship of creation, called to be God's ambassador on earth. Adam and Eve were entrusted as guardians of the world. To understand the role of Christ in His mission as the new Adam, to understand the role we have been given, we must understand the role that God had given Adam and Eve.

OUR FIRST IDENTITY

The Hebrew for guardian or steward is *Shomer*. The word carries a meaning that the English words "steward" and "guardian" struggle to capture. To be a *Shomer* is to be a legal guardian. In Jewish law, if someone is entrusted with the guardianship of an object, he is a *Shomer,* accountable to a rabbinical court if he does not discharge his responsibility. A Jew who keeps the Sabbath is known as *Shomer Shabbos.* Orthodox Jews who practice chastity by withdrawing from physical contact with the opposite sex are *Shomer Negiah.*

A *Shomer* is not just charged with guardianship, but also the responsibility to cultivate that which is in their care. For years the rabbis debated the problem of the *Shomer* of a basket of apples. Someone is made *Shomer* of a basket of apples by a friend. The apples start to go bad before the friend's return. What should the *Shomer* do? After consulting Scripture and much debate, the rabbis concluded that a *Shomer* should turn the apples into applesauce, instead of just letting them rot. Adam and Eve were not just charged with guardianship of the world, but were commanded to go forth and multiply, to work the soil, to exercise their role as image-bearers of God, creating as He creates. The *Shomer* cultivates that which is in his care. Yet after the fall, humankind is expelled from the garden. They find themselves wandering, lost, east of Eden. Like us today, they are not just geographically lost, but also lost to their true calling.

THE SERPENT THAT CREATED THE ROAD

How did it all fall apart? How did Adam and Eve lose their role as God's *Shomer*? The most obvious answer is that Eve and Adam ate of the fruit. Yet when we examine the story in depth, a key element emerges. Eve finds herself engaged in a conversation with the serpent. More than any other animal, the snake, cold to the touch, represents detachment. Some have noted that a snake when standing appears something like a question mark. Indeed it is a question that the snake poses, a deadly question that will tear apart the garden.

The serpent raises a possibility in the minds of Adam and Eve. Scripture tells us that creation was good, that humans lived in harmony with God and nature, knowing no pain or shame. Yet the serpent causes Adam and Eve to wonder if the grass is greener somewhere else, to wonder if God truly is good. The serpent's question in some ways is the ancestor of the culture of the road, which causes us to doubt the goodness of where we are at, to always be seduced by the possibilities over the horizon. Just like the culture of the road, the serpent also tempts us to break out from our divinely ordained place. The serpent is the first pagan, raising the possibility of there being more than one god, when he tells Eve that if she eats of the tree, that she and Adam may become like God.

> THROUGHOUT HISTORY, MANY WHO HAVE READ THIS STORY HAVE PAINTED EVE AS THE MAIN PLAYER IN THE FALL. YET A QUESTION MUST BE ASKED, WHAT IS ADAM DOING DURING THIS CONVERSATION?

HOW ADAM'S PASSIVITY TORE THE WORLD APART

Throughout history, many who have read this story have painted Eve as the main player in the fall. Yet a question must be asked, What is Adam doing during this conversation? One Jewish interpretation of this story portrays the conversation as a seduction. The serpent passed over as the potential *Shomer* plots to take over Adam's place, to be lord of the earth, with Eve his queen. Where is Adam as his wife is seduced, misled, entangled in a dialogue that she should not be having? Scripture alerts us to Adam's whereabouts with the simple phrase, "He was with her."[2] During the whole conversation, Adam is there, saying nothing, totally invisible. While his wife is misled, while his partner is seduced by the pagan lie that humans can be God, Adam the *Shomer*, charged with guardianship of creation, stands and does nothing. His silence speaks volumes. Many have commented that curiosity is Eve's sin, but passivity is the foundational sin of Adam.

Passivity is the polar opposite of God's intentions for His *Shomer.* Passivity is a mental and emotional withdrawing. Adam is physically present during the exchange with the serpent, yet for some reason, he has internally withdrawn. Adam is created by God to be engaged in relationship, primarily with God, then with Eve, and then with creation. It is Adam's passivity in these key relationships that creates the ground for withdrawal. Once one withdraws from relationship the potential for objectification arises. God's goodness can be questioned when one has withdrawn, creation can be used as a tool for personal advancement when one has begun to hold it at a distance. Adam can only let the serpent tempt and mislead his wife when he has emotionally and mentally withdrawn.

A few years ago I saw an interview with a security expert who advised companies when their employees were taken hostage in dangerous nations around the world. The interviewer asked him what the most important thing was that someone could do if they were taken hostage. His answer was strange—he said that you should start small talk. His advice was that you should ask the hostage taker about where they were born, their favorite things. You should start to tell your story, share seemingly mundane facts about yourself. The security expert said that the most important thing to do was to create a relationship that humanized you. He said that his years of experience in the field had taught him that murder is much easier when a person is seen simply as an object. When someone starts to build a relationship, to begin to know someone, the task of killing them is so much harder. The first step toward the Holocaust was the dehumanization of the Jews in the German media and popular culture. Cartoons portrayed Jews as rats, in propaganda films as subhuman. Only after the Nazis had turned the Jews into non-human objects in their minds could the killing begin.

Mental and emotional withdrawal inevitably leads to physical withdrawal. Adam's passivity leads to his expulsion from Eden, and the breaking of relationship with God, creation, and others. The passivity of Adam will make possible the murder of his son Abel.

The sin of passivity is also foundational to the culture of the road. While going on the road physically or mentally may seem like an active event, it is a withdrawal from everyday life, an escape from responsibility and a rejection of covenantal relationships. Hence the culture of the road has created a whole generation of young men who are essentially passive and reactive. Men who have learned not just to objectify women, but to objectify the whole of life, living at an ironic distance.

The culture of the road has created a world of objectification. It is only in an objectified world that millions can starve while we drown in a sea of fast food, gadgets, and stuff. It is only in an objectified world that fetuses can be aborted because of "lifestyle" choices. Only in an objectified world that reduces people into sexual objects can we be overrun with sexual crimes against women and children. Only in an objectified world can we vandalize God's creation, polluting our world and wiping out whole species.

Adam's passivity leads to withdrawal, which leads to distance, which leads to objectification, which leads to abuse, which leads to violence. This domino-like fall spreads out across the world, resulting in the evil that we read of in Genesis. Whereas Adam was passive, Abraham will be called to be active. Whereas Adam withdrew from relationship, God, and the world, Abraham will draw closer to God, move deeper into relationship with others, and take up the challenge to partner with God as He rebuilds the world. Thus God's reeducation of Abraham is a lesson in how to again take up the mantle of the *Shomer.*

EIGHTEEN:
LEAVING UR

To not pave the world, but instead to build gardens amongst the concrete...

Kerouac had stood in the shadow of his culture, pondering its power, wondering if there was another way. Millennia ago Abraham did the same. I like to imagine Abraham, looking every bit the madman, staring out into the frightening void of the dark desert. Feeling a pull, a powerful tow toward a nameless, unseen God. Behind him, all the might of the city, the walls of the grain storehouses. From the towering pyramid-shaped temple he can hear the drums, screams, and pagan chanting. In his gut, the doubt, the conflicting emotions, the fear that everything he has believed until now is wrong. The city represented safety, comfort, the known. In front of him, the desert representing death, darkness, mystery, and the unknown. Then the resolution, the determination, the trust, followed by the first step, away from the city, away from Ur. The first step of faith into the unknown, into the arms of God. The first step on a very different road.

WHY ABRAHAM WAS THE FIRST
COUNTERCULTURAL REBEL

Wading through books on Kerouac and the other Beat writers at the library, I picked up Ken Goffman's book *Counterculture through the Ages*. I knew of Goffman as a radical social activist and a champion of the counterculture, having read many of his articles during the '90s in the magazine *Mondo 2000*. Goffman's history of the counterculture included numerous mentions of Kerouac. I flipped to the beginning of the book to see who Goffman saw as the ancestor of Kerouac's countercultural stance. I almost swallowed my library card in surprise when I discovered Goffman's book, which includes chapters on Punk, LSD, the hippies, political revolutionaries, and Parisian bohemians, names biblical patriarch Abraham as one of the first countercultural icons.

Goffman reminds us that Abraham's life gives birth to a "religion of exile and dissent," that Abraham is "the leader of a small, dissenting minority living precariously on the margins of society."[1] An iconoclast, who takes a stand against a more powerful polytheistic society. Goffman quotes Rabbi Michael Lerner, who writes, "An idol worshipper named Abram revolutionized human history by trusting in a Being he could not see. Together with his wife Sarai, he left civilization behind and became a spiritual pioneer." There were similarities between Abraham and Kerouac. Both were known and defined by the journeys that they took. Both clearly show the limitations, failures, and frailties of being human. Kerouac and Abraham both make conscious decisions to chart alternative paths to the ones demanded of them by their cultures. Both choose to walk away from the mainstream. Both shape their lives around encounters they have with God.

As I read Goffman's chapter on Abraham, it dawned on me. Kerouac had illustrated a way of living, a mode of being that had helped to give birth to the spiritual and social mess that had followed. Abraham's life, however, offered another way of being human, another road. A way of being faithful, of living out one's faith, of leading the people of God that did not rely simply on better management, cooler graphics, or a finer sound system. So I began to again read Abraham's story, beginning with those simple, sparse words, which contained multitudes: "The Lord had said to Abram, 'Go from your country, your people and your father's household to the land I will show you.'"[2] When I got to the end of Abraham's story, I read it again. Each time I came to the conclusion and felt the need to move on to other parts of the Bible, I felt the call to go back and walk with him again, till his imprint was in my bones.

> WHEREAS AMERICANS VIEW THEIR CONTINENT AS BRIMMING WITH POTENTIAL, AUSTRALIANS HIDE FROM THE NOTHINGNESS IN THE CENTER OF OUR LAND, CLINGING TO THE COASTS.

Through the millennia, Abraham's example is shining a light into our secularized world. His life offers us another cultural code, another blueprint from which to live. He offers us a road of faith, in contrast to our culture's road of self.

THE SHOMER AND THE SONGLINES

My forehead presses agains the cool glass of the airplane window. I am flying across my continent, Australia. I look down and take in the endless red dirt, the utter absence of anything. I lose myself in my book for an hour, and look out the window again. The red dirt is still there, rolling on and on. Whereas Americans view their continent as brimming with potential, Australians hide from the nothingness in the center of our land, clinging to the coasts, hiding away in suburbs and cities. Our answer to Lewis and Clark, the Australian explorers Bourke and Wills, never return home; instead they die of starvation and exhaustion in the middle of the outback.

Whereas the European settlers of Australia would see a desert continent, and a vast land of nothingness, the Aboriginal people see a very different continent, viewing their land through a different set of eyes. For them, the land is covered in "songlines," pathways along which one travels singing aloud. The knowledge of these pathways was passed down through generations. Some songlines are short, others hundreds of miles, crisscrossing the continent like ancient unpaved roads, invisible to non-Aboriginal eyes. When I think of the Aboriginals walking their songlines I cannot but help think of Abraham walking out the land God has given him, as he learns again how to be the *Shomer* of creation.

Abraham has walked away from Haran with his nephew Lot in tow. His wealth and his entourage have grown. A dispute arises between Abraham and Lot's herders, and the two groups decide to separate in order to sustain their flocks. Abraham offers Lot his pick of the land. Lot looks out and sees the lush and fertile land of the plain, a plain the Bible likens to "the garden of the Lord, like the land of Egypt.[3]" This observation is critical. Having left Sumerian-Mesopotamian culture behind, the lure of the city still remains strong for the travelers. Lot, seeing this chance to return to what looks like Eden, claims the plain. Yet if the plain is like Eden, there must be a serpent somewhere in the midst of the lushness. The serpent's form this time is the city of Sodom, next to which Lot pitches his tents. A city which the Bible reminds us is marked by injustice, evil, and sinfulness. Lot is dazzled by the big city lights, he makes the crucial mistake of seeing things how they appear. The plain is an illusion, a mirage, its lushness purely superficial. Underneath its trees, strong city walls, and well-watered fields, evil lurks. The *Shomer* cannot again be seduced by the serpent, this time God's plan will be different.

Lot's decision to head off into the plain must have been particularly painful for Abraham. Having no son, Lot is his next of kin. In a culture that highly values heirs, Abraham has effectively said good-bye to his heir. His chance of continuing his legacy has seemingly been lost to the seductive fantasy offered by the plain. Abraham is told by the Lord that he and his offspring will be given all the land he can see. He is told by the Lord to go and walk the length and breadth of the Land. In the ancient world to claim land one only had to in the presence of a witness walk out the area that you were claiming, and then obviously you had to defend it. Imagine the sight of this old man, in the middle of the desert, alone walking out this land. Claiming it, not with a visible human witness, but with God as his witness. The *Shomer* will now be tasked with cultivating and bringing to life a desert instead of tending an established garden.

In contrast to the concrete securities and benefits of the plain and Sodom, Abraham's claiming of the land in earthly, visible terms is madness. Yet in God's unfolding plan, it makes perfect sense. Abraham is again asked to break with his culture, with the world, to walk to a different beat, to obey a set of rules that seemingly makes no sense. He is being asked again to walk the path of faith. Abraham's walking out of the land is a prophetic act, representing the life of the believer in an unbelieving world. An act that is just as relevant today as it was when Abraham walked out that land. So it is now up to you and me to leave Ur, to depart from Haran, to not be swayed by the lures of the lush valleys and their promises of Eden, but to go with Abraham, walk out the land that God has given us. To look out into a reduced world and see depth, to see life in a world that has reduced transcendence to consumer goodies. To pick up our once forgotten identities as the *Shomer* of creation, to not consume the world but to cultivate and create. To not pave the world with the asphalt of superhighways, but instead to build gardens amongst the concrete.

CHRIST THE COSMIC GARDENER

Whereas Abraham shows us how God began to teach humanity
how to again live as the *Shomer*, Christ's life, as the new Adam,
is our ultimate model of how to live as the *Shomer*. Mark's gospel
picks up the imagery of Christ as the new Adam, the *Shomer*.
Mark in his gospel writes, "He was in the wilderness forty days,
being tempted by Satan. He was with the wild animals, and angels
attended him."[4] Adam and Eve begin their ministry in the garden
of Eden, a utopian environment, and yet succumb to the serpent's
temptation. Christ begins His ministry in the wilderness, amongst
the staggering heat and sheer desolation of the Israeli desert. Yet
in this place He prevails against the devil's temptation. Adam and
Eve lose their special relationship with creation and are sent from
Eden, their way back blocked by the angels, their ministry in tatters. Christ moves into communion with the wild animals, served
by angels. He is not expelled from the wilderness but instead is
commissioned, sent to complete His ministry and mission.

We find Jesus living out His ministry on the road. He is always
walking, always moving. Like His ancestor Abraham, He is walking out the land, living out the kingdom that He is proclaiming, His
steps carving out Eden in the desert. His mobility is nothing like
our culture of the road, this journey has purpose and a destination. In John's gospel Jesus' role is made even clearer. Mary on
the morning of the resurrection mistakes Christ for a gardener.
This seemingly insignificant detail is crucial. John is telling us that
Jesus has become the cosmic gardener. Like a seed His body
is planted in the dead earth, planting the tree of life in the dead
earth, turning a graveyard back into Eden. He is now the *Shomer*,
fulfilling the mission, once given to Adam. He is a new kind of
human, representing what is to come, pulsating with life and the
holy. Reconnecting humanity with God, each other, and creation.

His resurrection a portent of the resurrection of creation.

Mary runs to tell the disciples that Christ has risen. In the next passage of John's gospel, the risen Jesus Himself appears to the disciples, showing them the scars in His hands. Saying to them, "Peace be with you! As the Father has sent me, I am sending you." And with that He breathed on them and said, "Receive the Holy Spirit." Just as God breathed the breath of life into Adam, Christ now breathes His breath into the disciples, giving them the Holy Spirit. Adam who was earth was brought to life by the breath of God, and now the disciples come to life in a new way. The disciples, so characterized by insecurity, jealousy, and confusion in the Gospels, are transformed. God's breath upon Adam was part of his commissioning as the *Shomer*, Christ's breath upon the disciples is also a commissioning. This breath comes with a responsibility. The disciples, those who follow, will become apostles, those who are sent. The Hebrew term for an apostle is *Shaliah*. A *Shaliah* is a *Shomer* with a mission.

> JUST AS GOD BREATHED THE BREATH OF LIFE INTO ADAM, CHRIST NOW BREATHES THE HIS BREATH INTO THE DISCIPLES, GIVING THEM THE HOLY SPIRIT.

SHOMER ON A MISSION

Whereas a *Shomer* is given charge of safeguarding and cultivating something for another, the *Shaliah* is an agent charged with a task. He is a proxy, fulfilling a duty for someone who is absent or unable to perform that obligation. Just as the *Shomer* is legally responsible for his duty of guardianship, so the *Shaliah* is responsible for his task of agency. The role of the *Shaliah* is traced back to Abraham. Seeking a wife for his son, Abraham sends out his servant to find a companion for Isaac. The servant is responsible for all of Abraham's property; he is the *Shomer* of Abraham's possessions. Abraham makes the servant take an oath, by placing his hand between Abraham's thighs. A symbolic act that some commentators have linked to the covenant of circumcision. Abraham's age prevents him from completing this task, so the servant becomes Abraham's proxy seeking out a wife for his son. The *Shomer* becomes the *Shaliah.* He who is responsible, who has the most important role in Abraham's household, is called to an even higher task. God's plan to redeem the world through Abraham's descendants is now in his hands. In the same way the disciples' role is expanded, as Jesus breathes upon them. They are no longer just *Shomer* charged with stewardship of the world they inhabit, they are given a new task, called to partner with God in the repairing of the world, in the uniting of heaven and earth.

Abraham's servant, the first *Shaliah*, is given the task of finding a bride who will continue God's plan. There is a parallel between this story and the task given to the apostles. To understand this parallel we must turn to the book of Revelation:

> I saw the Holy City, the new Jerusalem, coming down out of heaven from God, prepared as a bride beautifully dressed for her husband. And I heard a loud voice from the throne saying, "Look! God's dwelling place is now among the people, and he will dwell with them. They will be his people, and God himself will be with them and be their God. He will wipe every tear from their eyes. There will be no more death or mourning or crying or pain, for the old order of things has passed away."[5]

The passage speaks of the new heaven and the new earth. The completion of the redemption of creation as God come to live with humankind, the marriage of earth and heaven. The Bible begins with God dwelling in harmony with humankind, in the garden of Eden a place where there are no tears or death. The Bible ends with God returning to live in harmony with His people, again there are no tears or death. The old order in which the earth was overrun with evil, in which death and brokenness abounded, has passed. The New Jerusalem, the new Eden, is dressed resplendently for her husband. Thus the twelve are sent out as God's apostles, given His spirit as companion. They are now his *Shaliah*, charged with the task of bringing to Him His bride. Their role is to go out, on a very different road than the one chosen by our culture, uniting heaven and earth.

The apostles represent God's reengineering of humanity. In the garden of Eden, humankind's sin had torn apart the three key relationships of the cosmos. God to humans, human to human, and human to creation. The apostles are sent out in the world as messengers, announcing that Christ's death on the Cross has reconciled these three relationships. We too are sent. The details of our lives will differ, but our core calling is to go into the world, announcing through word and deed that God has repaired these three relationships. To find our way out of the impasse of the culture of the road, we must again return to our divinely given vocation in the world. Meaning and transcendence will only flow into our lives when we understand that Christ's death on the Cross has reconciled us to God, to others, and creation. When we live out of this truth, we can live lives of sacredness and meaning in a secular culture. The generations who come after Kerouac's cultural reprogramming must understand that we can only discover transcendence when we worship a transcendent creator God, instead of worshipping that which was created.

> TO FIND OUR WAY OUT OF THE IMPASSE OF THE CULTURE OF THE ROAD, WE MUST AGAIN RETURN TO OUR DIVINELY GIVEN VOCATION IN THE WORLD.

NINETEEN:
BREAKING INTO HEAVEN

Abraham and Sarah's barrenness was symbolic of the pagan worldview in which they lived...

The Sumerian-Mesopotamian world in which Abraham lived featured a strict and controlling worldview. Like our culture, it thoroughly misunderstood the divine. Archeologists have now discovered a number of creation myths from the areas in which Abraham lived, roughly situated in modern-day Iraq, which show us just how wrong they got it. The myths speak of capricious gods who create humans to be their cosmic slaves. In the myths, gods create the cities. These metropolises were not designed for human good but were giant factories designed to serve the appetite of insatiable gods, who, to keep the cosmos going, required huge agricultural offerings, as well as the "offerings" of temple prostitutes.

ANCIENT ECHOES OF THE SECULAR

Like our modern mythology of the road which never ends, the myths of Abraham's world contain no future point, no resolution upon which to hope. With no future hope, there was little chance of change. Heads were down, shoulders to the plow, everyone keeping the whole charade going, no one asking the dangerous question. The civilization that sprang up in the delta of the Tigris and Euphrates Rivers was the home of astrology. Human life was determined by the movement of distant heavenly bodies. This only added to the sense of fatalism present in Sumerian-Mesopotamian culture, a fatalism that we find present in our culture.

A deep vein of fear ran through Sumerian-Mesopotamian culture. It was unthinkable that the farmer would not get out of bed to tend his fields or that the temple prostitute would fail to perform her duties. To dare to question, to doubt, to not believe, let alone to walk away, was almost unthinkable. The entire force of culture, the weight of his world, pushed Abraham toward conformity, toward belief in the bloodthirsty, empty religion that fostered a brutal view of the world, justified slavery, crushed individuality, and valued vicious competition. Historian Thomas Cahill notes that the ancient Sumerians esteemed the powerful. Much exalted was the wild bull of a man who would humiliate and bully other men and sleep with scores of women. Cahill writes:

> Sumerian society . . . was intensely competitive, and Sumerians were swaggerers of the worst kind. Kings indulged in their own constant self-praise without a trace of inhibition. . . . This was a society full of contentiousness and aggression, in which the "good" man—the ideal—was imagined as ambitious in the extreme, animated by a drive for worldly prestige, victory, success, with scant regard to what we would think of as ethical norms. This was also a society that despised poverty.[1]

This was a society in which people were disposable and sex was a tool of power, mechanical and loveless. A two-dimensional world, devoid of imagination, filled with the functionality of paganism. The culture of Sumer-Mesopotamia was not secular by any stretch of the imagination. Its differences with our culture are immense. No doubt, however, you will be noticing the similarities. The parallels between our secular culture and Sumer-Mesopotamia's culture, both cynical, flattened, and devoid of life, make Abraham's choice to listen to an invisible God, to walk away from his society, all the more incredible, and all the more relevant to us in our quest to follow God in the secular West.

THE BARRENNESS OF THE ROAD

Abraham was hardly a starving discontent living on the bottom rungs of his culture. Genesis tells us that his family had settled for some time in Haran.[2] We are also told that Abraham had gathered an entourage of servants, and possessions, in Haran.[3] The book of Numbers tells us that Terah, Abraham's father was involved in the production of idols. Abraham's family was therefore deeply tied to the religious system of Sumer-Mesopotamia, no doubt Abraham's wealth was directly the result of his or at least his father's profiteering from paganism.

Yet despite the comfort that his culture had brought him, there was an incompleteness to his life. Scripture tells us that his wife Sarah was barren. Sarah's barrenness in Genesis is made all the more painful and poignant in that it is mentioned at the conclusion of a large genealogy, filled with children and fertile parents. Abraham and Sarah's inability to produce a child was a personal tragedy, but it was also symbolic of the barrenness of the worldview in which they lived, it alerts us to the sterility and unfruitfulness of paganism. Exposing its absolute inability to speak newness, to point to something outside of itself. The paganism of Abraham's world, just like the secularism of our world, offers us warmth, comfort, and familiarity, but ultimately it is barren. It offers us no mystery, nothing beyond, nothing sacred. In its impotency it cannot offer us redemption. In contrast, God's way, His promise, offers multitudes, bringing life to millions. Those who follow Abraham will be countless.

DEAD EARTH

To understand the radical nature of Abraham's walking away from his culture, to understand the road of faith, we must examine the story that appears just before Abraham's appearance in the book of Genesis. The shadow of the tower of Babel hangs over the story of Abraham, both must be read together:

> Now the whole world had one language and a common speech. As people moved eastward, they found a plain in Shinar and settled there. They said to each other, "Come, let's make bricks and bake them thoroughly." They used brick instead of stone, and tar for mortar.[4]

Humanity, expelled from paradise, continues its wandering, both in a physical and spiritual sense. The people move eastward, imitating Cain, who wanders away from the presence of God, always east of Eden. The temptation to resist this wandering, this lostness, is too much, and the people make the decision to settle. The great student of urbanism Lewis Mumford noted that in settling down and building the first cities, humans traded mobility for security. This is certainly true of the builders of Babel except they are not just seeking security, but a security apart from God. Mumford notes that nomads and wanderers were drawn to settle because of a desire to be near the burial grounds of their dead: "The city of the dead antedates the city of the living. In one sense, indeed, the city of the dead is the forerunner, almost the core, of every living city."[5] The desire to move on was quashed by a greater desire to be near the recently departed. The pain of the loss caused settlements and cities to spring up around the resting places of the departed. Perhaps the builders of Babel, separated from God, all too aware of death, decide to take control of their lives. To seek autonomy and beat death. To make a memorial to themselves. To try and beat the inevitable march of time.

THE CITY OF FEAR

Ernest Becker in his work *The Denial of Death*[6] made the charge that human culture is built upon a denial of our eventual deaths. This could not be more true of Babel. On one hand it is easy to understand the desire of Babel's inhabitants to stay in a place, to find shelter from a harsh world with the possible memory of the great flood hanging over them. One can understand their desire to build a high place, as high as the heavens, to avoid ever being flooded again. Ethicist Leon Kass, in his exploration of the book of Genesis, notes that Babel likely originated as a result of fear.[7] Kass observes that the inhabitants of Babel, in the aftermath of the great flood, have "better reason than most to know and fear nature's wildness and inhospitality and to shrink from standing unarmed and dispersed before the powers that be."[8] Fear, however, offers us a choice: to find security in God, or to seek security in our own strength. The builders of Babel attempt the latter and by doing so, usurp the place of God. The first clue that informs us of their decision is their choice of building materials. The seemingly mundane observation that the builders chose to fire their own bricks, rather than build with stone, is key.

To build and use stone is to work with already fashioned materials, to construct under God's mandate of being stewards of the creation, working within God's parameters for being human. Instead the builders chose to mimic God, who used soil to create Adam. But instead of taking living soil and breathing life into it, the builders place soil into fire, burning it thoroughly. The living soil, filled with potential, is made lifeless. A brick has been created—the perfect tool for human manipulation, the building block of the rebellion against God. Leon Kass writes:

> In creating man, God had breathed life into the ruddy earth ('adamah') to create adam, the ruddy earthling. In contrast, the earthlings here burn the ruddy earth into ghostly and lifeless (white) brick: the word for brick, levenah, comes from a root, lavan, meaning "white." In this subtle way, the text already hints that man's creative project is in fact a reversal of God's creation of man, and that its results may well be deadly.[9]

Humans, created in the image of God, have the power to act within God's will. Or we have the choice to go it alone, trying to gain meaning, through attempting to create the good life in our own strength. To burn our own bricks. R. R. Reno, reflecting on the story of Babel,[10] notes that humanity faces a clear choice, a choice between the covenant of life and the covenant of the lie. The story of the burnt bricks is a warning to us. We carry with us a dreadful power that is the touch of death—just as the burning of the bricks robbed the soil of life, reducing it to a white, deathly remnant of itself, a tool to be exploited. When we live under our own autonomy, cut off from God's will, we bring that deathly touch to all that we encounter. We see this everywhere in our culture today, almost every aspect of human life is burnt, reduced, and objectified. Relationships are to be exploited, the poor are dehumanized, sexuality is reduced to mechanics, creation is misused and turned into a garbage dump. The city aids this manipulation of life. For the city is self-contained; it provides for all of its citizens' needs. Babel is a closed world, Leon Kass writes:

> In Babel . . . the dream of the city holds full sway in the hearts and minds of its inhabitants. Protected by its walls, warmed and comforted in its habitats, and ruled by its teachings, the children of Adam, now men of the city, neither know nor seek to know anything beyond.[11]

The culture of the West is also a closed world. Driving across the expansive state of South Dakota, I looked out the window to see a vast canvas of stars. On the lonely highway, the heavenly display conveys to me a sense of cosmic smallness, a sense of wonder that pointed my thoughts to a God who is more powerful than us. A handful of days later, I am standing in the chaos of Times Square, in the heart of Manhattan. All around me a buzz of people, each with their own agendas. Unlike the farmer in South Dakota, their gaze is not upwards to the stars, and onwards to the transcendent. Rather it is heads down, each consumed in their own universes of self. The subways provide rabbit holes to dive into. The brightness of the stores, the billboards, and the skyscrapers cannot but distract. Who needs stars when you have the bright lights of the city?

THE CITY OF BABEL IS THE FIRST HUMAN EXPERIMENT IN DENYING THE TRANSCENDENT.

The city of Babel is the first human experiment in denying the transcendent and attempting life completely within the immanent. Its roots are our culture's roots; the spirit of the builders of Babel is present within us. With no transcendent truth, the city of Babel cannot look to any outside knowledge of justice and common good. The city then becomes a threat, not only to its citizens, but to God's plan for the world. Christian sociologist Jacques Ellul noted that "it is only in an urban civilization that man has the metaphysical possibility of saying, 'I killed God.'"[12] Babel, like our culture, with its immanent focus, has the potential to launch a full-scale attack upon God.

STORMING HEAVEN

As we earlier established, to understand Abraham, we must understand that which he decides to walk away from. Here the story of God's intervention in the building of the tower of Babel is crucial. We noted that Babel was established in a climate of fear, leading to the creation of a city, which promised security and comfort apart from God. Babel for its inhabitants meant that there would be no more wandering, that nature could be repelled, that technology could promise humans mastery. Emboldened by their newfound knowledge of brick making, the people decide to build "a tower that reaches to the heavens, so that we may make a name for ourselves; otherwise we will be scattered over the face of the whole earth."[13]

The desire of the builders of Babel to make a name for themselves is enlightening. To make a name for oneself is to be remembered for posterity. The culture of the fear of death that Babel has been built upon creates a desire in its inhabitants to seemingly beat death, a passion to be known through a feat of daring. Like the celebrity culture of our day, the builders seek to conquer mortality by being known by the masses. Like our culture of the road it is a bold attempt to shape their world, to carve transcendent meaning out of the immanent through a force of will.

By seeking to make a name for themselves, the people are mimicking God. God gave humans their name, thus indicating His power over them. In turn God gave humans the power to name the animals, indicating their status as stewards of creation. What the builders of Babel desire is to rename themselves. That is, to gain autonomy, to escape the laws and boundaries of God's created order. Not wanting to simply worship God's transcendence, the builders of Babel attempt to appropriate transcendence for themselves. The builders of Babel wish to re-create themselves.

This is the sin of the road, an attempt to escape our context, to transcend ourselves through a force of will, to remake ourselves. This attempt at re-creation is the oldest sin, it is the sin of Adam and Eve, who give in to the serpent's temptation to become like God. Rabbi Jonathan Sacks notes that:

> The builders of Babel were in effect saying: we are going to take the place of God. We are not going to respond to His law or respect His boundaries, not going to accept His Otherness. We are going to create an environment where we rule, not Him, where the Other is replaced by Self.[14]

Rabbi Sacks links the desires of the builders of Babel and the philosophy of Nietzsche, who re-invoked the spirit of Babel in the nineteenth century. We can see this spirit, this desire to make a name for ourselves through our Nietzchean attempts to carve meaning into life—to, in essence, become mini-gods. "When human beings try to become more than human, they quickly become less than human," observes Rabbi Sacks, pointing out that Nietzsche's vision of being human came only three quarters of a century before the inhuman slaughter of sons and daughters of Abraham in the Holocaust. At the heart of the pagan city of Babel, notes Rabbi Sacks, is the desire to traverse God-given limits.

But God will radically intervene in the world, in the life of one man. Birthing out of this man, and his family, a whole new way of being human, one that repairs the broken world. Yet for such an encounter to occur, the human heart must be rid of its pagan heart, through an encounter with a transcendent God.

TWENTY:

HOW GETTING GOD RIGHT CHANGES EVERYTHING

At moments of loss and tragedy
we turn to the faraway god . . .

In some ways I have painted a potentially contradictory picture of the worldview of the culture of the road. On one hand we wish for a Godless reality, looking for meaning in the immanent, and on the other hand looking for a greater sense of meaning, a force in the cosmos that tells us that our lives matter, a god who will offer us a chance at the eternal. How can this be so? Richard Keyes' insights on the nature of idols offer us a key to understanding this contradictory approach to belief. The Sumerian-Mesopotamian culture featured two levels of gods. Keyes makes the observation that idols come in pairs. First there is the nearby idol, which is a result of human need for dominion, control, and autonomy. These nearby idols offer humans a sense of well-being, the feeling that they can control their everyday lives. They relate to the immanent realm, aiding humans in the everyday realms of sexuality, relationships, finances, and health. They are immediate and tangible, realms that we feel we can manipulate and control.

TWO IDOLS. TWO GODS.

In our contemporary culture we are knee-deep in nearby idols. They are not just made of stone and wood; today they stare back at us from catalogues, TV screens, and our laptop displays. The sheer amount of nearby idols on display today would make a Sumerian priest blush. In our immanence-obsessed culture, almost everything within reach is transformed into an idol.

Keyes crucially observes that nearby idols cannot give our lives "a sense of meaning, coherence of life, or ultimate safety."[1] Thus the adherent of a nearby idol must seek a sense of the transcendent in another kind of idol. The nearby idol cannot give a sense of the transcendent without the worshipper losing the sense of control and autonomy that makes the nearby idol attractive in the first place. A sense of the transcendent can only be found in what Keyes names the "faraway" idol. The Sumerian-Mesopotamian culture had its immanent gods the Marduks and Baals, but it also had the faraway god El the benign, who had created the world and, as his name suggests, was portrayed as benevolent, but unable to offer the tangible goodies that the nearby idol could. The faraway god offers a loose sense of coherence, of meaning without burdening the worshipper with a comprehensive set of expectations or morals to follow. Keyes notes that today for secular people, the faraway god could be a loosely held belief, such as the belief in progress, destiny, luck, or a universal belief in love.

Keyes' insight helps us understand how many in our culture can hold to a fuzzy kind of belief in God, yet also simultaneously act like atheists. It helps us grasp the contradictory approach to faith that is so prevalent in our society. Our current reduced secular worldview is the perfect factory for the creation of nearby gods. We turn consumer goods, sex, technology, travel, experience, and career into idols—idols that are attempts to create modules of meaning in an empty, transcendence-free universe. Thus the supposed gods of our age, our idols, are, in the words of theologian David Bentley Hart, "merely masks by means of which the one true god—the will—at once conceals and reveals itself." The real nearby gods, then, are—ourselves. The only idol that we bow down to, the only god to whom we are unequivocally devoted to, is ourselves. Thus we stomp through life like angry and restless toddlers, attempting to satiate our desires, to gain transcendence from that which is immanent, to master that which cannot be controlled.

We exhaust the world, wanting to worship that which was never designed to be worshipped, and to be worshipped ourselves. Our lives become stuck in a loop, and thus contemporary life is marked by a constant wanting more, ever-present dissatisfaction, and restlessness. Our lives are marked by a constant wandering; a fluidity concerning relationships, careers, home, sexuality, identity, and belief is now the norm. Such a restlessness inevitably at times leads us to a desire for the transcendent. At moments of loss and tragedy, when the existential questions break through the chatter and the buzz, we turn to the faraway god. This faraway idol is a god in name only, a deity robbed of its power to truly intervene in the world, to offer justice, salvation, and redemption; instead it just offers soppy sentimentalisms. It can only give us saccharine visions of heaven, and temporary spiritual solace. The loose and fuzzy faraway god cannot give us what we really need, it cannot offer us a sense of ethics and justice, it cannot tell us that we are not the center of the universe, that we are not god. Because at the end of the day the faraway idol, the distant god, is really just a complicit player in fantasy that we are gods, the ultimate authority lies with us.

WALT DISNEY IN A ROBE

Sadly, we can see the nearby and faraway gods at work in contemporary Christianity. Jesus is ripped from His position and recast as the nearby god, reshaped by our culture expectations, robbed of His countercultural essence. Instead He is turned into a deliverer of dreams, a magician of wish fulfillment, Walt Disney with a beard and robe, making our twenty-first-century consumer dreams come true. Or, He is recast as a permissive hipster, a laid-back spiritual guru, not hung up on whether we really follow Him, someone like "The Dude" in the Coen brothers film *The Big Lebowski*. Others turn Him into the therapist, quietly listening to our droning, completely obsessed with and attentive to our emotional state, a professional assistant in our quest for well-being. Never asking us to do anything—just simply and benignly listening to us.

> GOD THE FATHER MAKES US UNCOMFORTABLE BECAUSE INTUITIVELY WE KNOW THAT ALL AUTHORITY RESTS WITH HIM.

The Holy Spirit can also be misinterpreted as a nearby idol, purely existing to offer us experiential ticklings that do not lead us to repentance, personal transformation, or mission. This immanetized version of the Holy Ghost is our tool, contained and domesticated. It obediently turns up at the right moments, the apex of the worship service, or the altar call of the youth camp. God the Father then becomes the faraway god. We are uncomfortable with the aura of justice around Him, so we hold Him at arm's length, confining Him to His role as the creator of the world, or the "God" of the Old Testament, preferring Jesus of the Gospels. All the while forgetting that two thousand years of Christian teaching has affirmed that Jesus was God in human form. God the father makes us uncomfortable not because He is evil, frightening, or a tyrant, but because intuitively we know that all authority rests with Him. By acknowledging this truth, we admit that we are not in charge, that the created cannot rule over the creator. Only an encounter with the true transcendence of God can free us from our confused and debilitating self-rule.

The otherworldly nature of God was communicated powerfully to Abraham as he journeyed to Mount Moriah, ready to offer his son. After years of Abraham holding on to God's promise for an heir, God had delivered to him a boy named Isaac. Yet one day this developing relationship between Abraham and God seemingly changes. God asks Abraham the impossible, to take his son to Mount Moriah and sacrifice him as a burnt offering to God. Such a story today fills us with horror. In our culture where those who harm children are considered the lowest of the low, such a passage has had critics calling God a child abuser. Yet when we understand its context, the passage takes on a different hue. To grasp this nuance we need to understand the way that God differed from the other gods of the time. Especially the god Moloch.

FEEDING YOUR CHILDREN TO MOLOCH

The crowd was jammed into San Francisco's Six Gallery like sardines. Kerouac, drunk, joined in the cheering, roaring his friend Allen Ginsberg on as he read his now legendary poem *Howl.* The initially reluctant Ginsberg, now feeding off the energy of the crowd, shed his insecurity and began to roar like a beatnik Jeremiah,

Moloch! Solitude! Filth! Ugliness! Ashcans and unobtainable dollars! Children screaming under the stairways! Boys sobbing in armies! Old men weeping in the parks!

Moloch whose eyes are a thousand blind windows! Moloch whose skyscrapers stand in the long streets like endless Jehovahs! Moloch whose factories dream and croak in the fog!

Moloch whose smokestacks and antennae crown the cities!

Moloch! Moloch! Robot apartments! invisible suburbs! skeleton treasuries! blind capitals! demonic industries! spectral nations! invincible mad houses! monstrous bombs![2]

Howl deliberately referenced the name of the ancient god Moloch, one of the collection of localized deities worshipped in the ancient Near East. Moloch's notoriety comes from the cult of child sacrifice that was attached to his worship. Early Jewish commentaries speak of Moloch being worshipped as a brass idol with hollow drawers, drawers in which animals and other offerings would be placed, in the final drawer a child would be offered. The brass idol would be heated, and the drums would beat to drown out the screams of the child.

The sacrifice of one's child must have been an act of desperation, an attempt to forestall a loss of crops or to avert a famine. Even later in Israel's history, the people of God, when in dire circumstances, must have been tempted to revert to the worship of Moloch. The book of Leviticus reads, "Do not give any of your children to be sacrificed to Molek, for you must not profane the name of your God. I am the Lord."[3] As Abraham set out on his journey, it would have been entirely conceivable to him that a deity would request a child as sacrifice. The idea might be terrible, yes, but also expected.

Ancient hearers of this story would anticipate that the story would end with Abraham sacrificing Isaac as an offering to his god. The shock in the story for ancient readers would not be that God would ask Abraham to sacrifice his child, but that God would not allow Abraham to sacrifice his child. God does test Abraham, but God is also tested. The story raises a question, "Is God like Moloch?" The answer is clear: He is not. This God is nothing like the gods of Abraham's world. He does not devour that which is most precious. He does not ask that we sacrifice our futures for the sake of the present. God cannot be controlled by the popular imagination of the day. This story, so strange, so foreign, fits like a round peg in a square hole in our contemporary understanding — reminding us that the God who will save us transcends our human agendas and contemporary sensibilities.

THE MODERN MOLOCH

Ginsberg had linked Moloch to contemporary secularized culture, a culture which offered consumer items and a high standard of living but worked against spirituality and the transcendent. It is inevitable that our culture will influence our view of God. In our age Moloch is far from dead. From outside of the Church, cultural critic Barbara Ehrenreich offers a scorching evaluation of how a traditional Christian view of God has been subverted by the contemporary self.

Ehrenreich notes that teachings centered on the idea of a transcendent God, whose desire is that we turn from sin, have been abandoned in the contemporary Christian climate by many leaders who have been "willing to abandon traditional Christian teachings insofar as they might be overly challenging or disturbing."[4] In the place of theology rooted in a transcendent God, Ehrenreich laments the rise

> WE SACRIFICE GOD'S FUTURE OF PROMISE AND POTENTIAL FOR GRATIFICATION IN THE MOMENT.

of what she labels "positive theology," in which the contemporary self can bully God through a force of will into delivering results in the immediate. The gospel, according to Ehrenreich, is distorted into the message, "You can have all that stuff in the mall, as well as the beautiful house and car, if only you believe that you can." Such a view of God "ratifies and completes a world without beauty, transcendence, or mercy."[5] When we re-imagine God as a facilitator of our personal dreams, or a deliverer of consumer goods, we turn Him into Moloch. We sacrifice God's future of promise and potential for gratification in the moment.

GOD AS PEERANT

Often our view of God is influenced by our view of our parents. The baby boomers, obsessed with the generation gap, defined themselves against authoritarian father figures. As the baby boomers became parents themselves, they found themselves in a bind, they were now the authority. The first youth culture was no longer youth. So a great re-envisioning of parenthood began. A more permissive mode of parent would evolve. The authoritarian view of the parent, held by most cultures since the dawn of time, was replaced with the "peerant." Discipline, responsibility, and boundaries were out; relating, the development of self-esteem, and ethical flexibility was in.

Unlike previous generations who had fallen into the trap of viewing God like their stern, distant fathers, today we are more likely to imagine God as something akin to a permissive mother. The Mom, who would drop anything to come and give you a life, who would pay for all of your breakages, write you sick notes when you took a day off school, and who let you eat chocolate just before bed because you threw a tantrum. When you view God as a permissive mother, it is natural that the universe will become morally insignificant. Faith will become a favor to God. Devotion and worship will be transformed into an expectation of entertainment and a desire for reward.

TWENTY-ONE:
HOLY VANDALISM

Christ's death on the cross shatters the mythology that our choices do not matter...

Before we can truly grasp the reality of the sovereignty and majesty of God, we must destroy the idols and imitations of God that command our worship.

THE HOLY HAMMER

There is a rabbinical tale that features the young Abraham, working in Haran for his father in his idol-selling business. Abraham's doubt concerning the power of the idols is growing. He begins to mock customers, asking one older idol worshipper how he can bow before something that is only a day old. One morning, Abraham has the job of placing before his father's collection of idols offerings of meat. Dramatically moved by the Spirit of God and enraged by his culture's devotion to idols, Abraham takes a hatchet and smashes them to pieces. Panicking at what he has done, Abraham cheekily places the hatchet in the hands of one of the larger gods.

Terah, enraged, finds his son, accusing him of the blasphemous act of vandalism. Abraham tells his father that the destruction was not caused by his hand, but rather was the result of the larger god, who became violent when meat was unevenly distributed. Terah, now angry at his son's attempt to frame one of his idols, tells his son that he created the idols with his own hands, out of stone and wood, and thus knows beyond a doubt that they have no voice, no actions, no power, no life. Abraham then cuttingly asks how his father can worship that which contains no power. It is a perfect "gotcha" moment. Both the idols' lifelessness and Terah's doubt are exposed for all to see. This healthy iconoclasm will be the double-edge to faith.

Abraham is called the father of faith, but he marks the first steps in what will be a journey of appropriate doubt, a skepticism that will mark Israel and the people of God. From Moses' mocking the power of Pharaoh, to Ezekiel humiliating the prophets of Baal, to Jesus' chastening of the Pharisees, to the early Church's resistance to the idolatry of the Roman Empire, biblical spirituality mocks and undermines anything that attempts to elevate itself above its God-given station, reserving its greatest scorn for that which takes the place of God.

Let's not dress this up. This is not detached cynicism. This is a criticism that costs. It is this skepticism that saw prophets killed and the early Christians thrown to the lions. It has provided much fuel to the blaze of anti-Semitism, and is the reason why today there are believers sitting in prison cells across the world.

THE ANTI-IDOL

Abraham's journey takes him as far as the great tree of Moreh. I always find this mention of a tree strange, an allusion perhaps to the Tree of Life left behind by humanity in the garden. Humans cannot reclaim their place in the garden by a show of force—a Babel-like storming of heaven. Humanity's path is not back to Eden but toward God's future. When he reaches the tree, Abraham creates an altar.

An altar is very different from an idol. An idol is a human creation, inevitably shaped by its maker's imagination or experience, a three-dimensional representation of their fears and/or desires. The idol maker tries to bring the transcendent into the immanent, shaping the divine into a recognizable form. Even if the idol worshipper bows, brings offerings, and offers worship facedown before the object, the power still lies with the idol maker. Creator cannot worship creation. The idol is ultimately a tool of the idol maker, their effort to influence what they cannot and should not. It is an attempt to be godlike. In contrast, Abraham's empty altar is stunningly radical, marking a return to the worship of the one true God. Its emptiness speaks volumes. It honors a God who cannot be fashioned by human hands. With no image the human cannot be creator. The power balance is correct. The idol cannot be manipulated, bribed, or coerced. Here Abraham, in the immanent, is focused on the transcendent God.

GOD AS "OTHER"

Abraham's appreciation of and encounter with the female "other" of Sarah will lay the groundwork for his numerous encounters with the other that is God. Tellingly, Scripture states that Sarah is beautiful. This is something we are used to; almost every leading lady in television or movies today is attractive. Yet this mention of beauty in the context of Abraham's culture carries with it a very different meaning. We know that the culture of Sumer-Mesopotamia was functional, based on fertility, a giant fear-driven machine designed to keep the universe going. Sex was mechanical, an animalistic, masculine show of force. In contrast, Abraham's

"IF WE HAVE NEVER HAD THE EXPERIENCE OF TAKING OUR CASUAL, RELIGIOUS SHOES OFF OUR CASUAL, RELIGIOUS FEET—GETTING RID OF ALL THE EXCESSIVE INFORMALITY WITH WHICH WE APPROACH GOD—IT IS QUESTION-ABLE WHETHER WE HAVE EVER STOOD IN HIS PRESENCE."

love is not grounded in the world of fertility and power, but rather mutual love and attraction to "the other."

His love and his appreciation for her beauty are the first, embryonic signs of a philosophic love, an attraction and a love that is founded in a desire for the transcendent. In its purest form, romantic love is an attraction to the other, that which we cannot be. Of course we appreciate similar interests and commonalities in those that we are attracted to—they provide the common ground of friendship. Yet it is that which is different in the other that produces passion, or erotic love. Men are attracted to that in the feminine which is different, and vice versa. In the same way, we are initially drawn to Christ due to what is familiar about Him, yet it is what is strange and different about Him that produces devotion within us. Oswald Chambers once observed:

If we have never had the experience of taking our casual, religious shoes off our casual, religious feet—getting rid of all the excessive informality with which we approach God—it is questionable whether we have ever stood in His presence. The people who are flippant and disrespectful in their approach to God are those who have never been introduced to Jesus Christ. Only after the amazing delight and liberty of realizing what Jesus Christ does, comes the impenetrable "darkness" of realizing who He is.

When God stopped the sacrifice of Isaac, Abraham under-stood that he was dealing with a very different kind of God. This was not a localized deity, the god of a city or mountain; this was the God of the universe. This was a God who was relational, who called out to Abraham by name the way one would call out to their child, yet who was also strange, and surprising. As God rebuilds His world through His interactions with this ancient nomad, Abraham must again learn what God is like. Adam and Eve walked with God in the garden of Eden. We, like Abraham, must rediscover God anew. Our hunger for transcendence can only be satiated by a transcendent God. The world can only be made sacred again by understanding the utter sacredness of God. Awe and mystique will only touch our lives when we worship a God who is mysterious and awesome. We can only worship a God who is wholly other, otherwise our faith will simply be an exercise in narcissism.

Instead of trying to erase the frictions between our culture and the God of Scripture we must hold them, despite how uncomfortable they may be. Christian author Andrew Shamy writes:

> The God of the Bible is deeply troubling, he constantly refuses to be placed in our comforting boxes. He is a God, like C.S. Lewis's Aslan, who is good, but wild. Those parts of scripture that shock us, the portrayals of God's holiness, otherness, distance, mystery, wrath and sometimes silence are so important; they remind us that God *is* God, we don't get to make him whoever we want him to be.[1]

When we meet such a wild God, He is not reshaped in our image, instead we are reshaped. God held Abraham's son in His hand and showed mercy. This transcendent God would prove on Mount Moriah that He was wild, but that He was also good, He was not Moloch. Yet on Calvary, we would become Moloch. The descendants of Abraham would hold God's Son in our hand and show no mercy. Humanity instead of ministering grace would kill.

Despite the murder of Christ, the transcendent God would

choose to take upon Himself the sufferings and pain of humanity. This God who was wholly other would offer Himself as a living sacrifice for the sins of His children. An encounter with such a God can only reshape us, and fill us with awe. Next to such a God our petty travels on the road, our attempts to enforce our wills on the world, to make our little dreams happen, seem utterly pitiful. When we follow a wild God, our view of life cannot remain the same, life becomes filled with a sense of importance.

WHY OUR CHOICES REALLY MATTER

A recent article in *Relevant* magazine[2] noted that 80 percent of evangelical unmarried American young adults have had sex. Reacting to the findings, Christian experts and commentators offered their opinions, noting the role of sex in the media, the delaying of marriage, and the role of the abstinence movement. Yet I believe such a statistic tells us more about our beliefs about the universe than it does about our sex drives. It reveals that we have fallen for a secular view of the cosmos in which our choices really do not matter.

The fact that God would choose to die for our sins illustrates just how important our choices in this world are. In our secular culture, which reduces everything to a joke, which sees nothing as sacred, which views the universe as a morally insignificant place, Christ's death on the Cross shatters the mythology that our choices do not ultimately matter, that our actions are inconsequential. When we choose to follow a transcendent God, when we rearrange our lives around His death on a Cross, we find ourselves back in a universe that is morally significant. Christian Smith and Melinda Lundquist Denton write:

> Such a universe means that one's single modest life is at another level also inescapably bound up to a larger framework

of consequence. In a morally significant universe, one's decisions and practices and deeds bear the burden and reflect the significance of a much bigger story. . . . In such a reality, moral temptations are serious business, as choices for right and wrong reverberate far beyond our own lives and affirm or violate a larger cosmic order.[3]

To contemplate a morally significant universe is to find one's sense of radical autonomy diminishing, our life on the road in tatters. All of a sudden everything matters. The thought that all of our actions, attitudes, and decisions cosmically count is terrifying. Yet this is exactly the place we need to be in. A place in which we desperately need grace.

The Polish poet Czeslaw Milosz, after living under both Nazi and Communist regimes, came to the conclusion that the horror of the modern era was rooted in the "belief in nothingness after death—the huge solace of thinking that for our betrayals, greed, cowardice, murders we are not going to be judged."[4] This is true not just of totalitarian regimes but also the contemporary West. It is revealing that many today hold on to a belief in heaven, but wish to ditch the idea of hell or eternal consequences for our wrongdoing. The morally significant universe is a place according to Milosz where "our deeds are imperishable." The only being in the world with the power to wipe the slate of our actions clean is He who is beyond our control.

The morally significant universe drives us away from ourselves and back to God. It is a reminder that our actions echo throughout eternity, that there are eternal consequences to the attitudes of our hearts. Such a belief lays the foundation for a very different kind of faith—a faith nothing like Moral Therapeutic Deism, Christian Agnosticism, or pop spirituality. Instead such a faith produces devotion and discipleship. Such a faith is not controlled by fear or guilt, but rather by awe and gratitude. An encounter with the transcendent God who is wholly other, cannot but create humility and devotion in us.

THE LANDSCAPE OF DEVOTION

In 1994 William Dalrymple went on the road to write his book *From the Holy Mountain*. Dalrymple did not travel across the United States like Kerouac but took a very different route, visiting the dying Christian communities of the Middle East. Dalrymple found a once-mighty world of faith that was desperate and disappearing. In the face of social isolation and persecution the Christians of the Middle East are migrating to Brazil, Germany, and Australia. There are now more Jerusalem-born Christians in Sydney than in Jerusalem. The book is a lament, a depressing and distressing account of the Church's fate within the Muslim world.

> THE MORE I READ OF THE STORIES OF THE CHRISTIANS OF THE MIDDLE EAST THE MORE I WAS TOUCHED BY THEIR UTTER DEVOTION. SOME OF THE PRIESTS AND MONKS KNEW THAT DEATH WAS NOT JUST A POSSIBILITY BUT AN INEVITABILITY, AND YET STILL CONDUCTED THEIR SERVICES IN WORSHIP OF CHRIST.

Dalrymple visited churches that have been bombed, whose priests have been killed, whose congregations have fled—yet who still continue to operate in the most dangerous of circumstances. With my Protestant background, and as someone raised around the Church Growth movement, the idea of a priest in flowing black robes, conducting a service for a handful of people in an ancient church where Christ had been worshipped for over a millennium, seemed an exercise in futility. Yet the more I read of the stories of the Christians of the Middle East the more I was touched by their utter devotion. Some of the priests and monks knew that death was not just a possibility but an inevitability, and yet still conducted their services in worship of Christ.

In one Lebanese valley, Dalrymple comes upon an ancient old man who stares at him warily from a grove of trees. In a low voice the old man asks if Dalrymple is a Christian. Dalrymple nods, and the old man beckons him, grasping his hand. The old man leads him to his hut, which is attached to a small chapel. Dalrymple discovers that the old man is the only Christian priest left in the valley. Each day he worships alone in the tiny chapel, his only audience God. Dalrymple, concerned for the man's well-being, asks if his life is a happy one.

The old man pauses before replying, "Yes it is happy, but only because it is difficult."[5] Despite the loneliness and depression the old man experiences, he shares his sense of "the indescribable joy of feeling the presence of the Lord." Dalrymple before departing asks the old priest if he will emigrate to escape the violence like so many others. The old man replies, "Whatever happens, I will stay. I am a prisoner of God. I cannot leave this place." How different an attitude from the one we find today in our culture of the road! I wonder how many believers in the West would describe themselves as prisoners of God?

We do not live in war-torn environments; our lives are not endangered because of our beliefs. Yet I believe that the devotion of the Christians in the Middle East to God is a witness to us in the West. Upon visiting Israel, Dalrymple asks the Patriarch of Jerusalem his opinion on the viability of Christianity in the Middle East. The Patriarch wisely reflects, "Do not judge a light by the size of its container. Even a small oil lamp can give light to a big room." Dalrymple's journey is not just geographic; it is a journey across a landscape of devotion.

When I reflect upon the Patriarch's words, I believe that they apply not only to the Middle East but to the West. Maybe we need to stop looking at the quantity of those who claim to follow and start looking to the quality of the devotion of our hearts.

HEAVENLY WORSHIP IN THE SECULAR CITY

My home, Melbourne, is a growing, cosmopolitan, and vibrant city of four million people. It is currently rated the world's most livable city, while Australia is rated the world's best medium-size country. Believers here do not face persecution or violence. Yet in this city only 2 percent of eighteen- to thirty-five-year-olds are actively engaged in faith. Theological heavyweights Stanley Hauerwas and D. A. Carson have both commented on the power of secularism in Australia not so much because the government represses faith, but because life here is just so comfortable. Mark Driscoll noted upon visiting Australia that the Church here faces a challenge because life here is a little bit too much like heaven. In such a place with its landscape of comfort, we can learn from the landscape of devotion of the remaining Christians in the Middle East. Only a wholehearted following of a transcendent God can create devotion in the comfortable West.

In the book of Revelation we encounter the risen, transcendent Christ. John writes:

When I turned I saw seven golden lampstands, and among the lampstands was someone like a son of man, dressed in a robe reaching down to his feet and with a golden sash around his chest. The hair on his head was white like wool, as white as snow, and his eyes were like blazing fire. His feet were like bronze glowing in a furnace, and his voice was like the sound of rushing waters. In his right hand he held seven stars, and coming out of his mouth was a sharp, double-edged sword. His face was like the sun shining in all its brilliance. When I saw him, I fell at his feet as though dead. Then he placed his right hand on me and said: "Do not be afraid. I am the First and the

*Last. I am the Living One; I was dead, and now look, I am alive
for ever and ever! And I hold the keys of death and Hades."*[6]

After the earthiness of Jesus in the Gospels, this portrayal of
Christ comes as a shock. The Jesus who sat with the woman at
the well, who ate with tax collectors, and who loved the presence of children seems very different from this heavenly entity.
The Christ described by John in his apocalypse is wholly other.
John can only fall at Christ's feet as if he were dead. Reflecting
on this passage, biblical commentator Joseph
Mangina writes that such an image renders
Christ "strange to us, bringing the reader/hearer
into his awesome presence, and forcing us to
confront the unparalleled claim he makes on our
lives."[7] Such a claim coupled with a vision of Christ's transcendence means that we cannot come before Him with the casual-
ness that contemporary culture breeds into us. Such a vision
demands that our worship and Christian devotion must differ from
the general attitude of the day.

**WE LIVE IN A CULTURE
WHERE WE WORSHIP
HOW AND WHEN IT
SUITS US.**

Older readers may wince at such a suggestion, thinking back
to Sunday church services filled with guilt, coercion, and stodgy
traditionalism. Yet most young adults have come of age in a very
different era within the Church. Recently while guest speaking
at a church, I asked the minister how many people would be in
attendance. He replied wryly, "Anywhere between one hundred
and fifty and three hundred. You just can't tell anymore these
days." We live in a culture where we worship how and when it
suits us. Another pastor from a church well known for its innovative approach to ministry shared with me that despite his church's
growth, there had been a sharp decline in those contributing their
time, ministry, and finances—that despite the church's public
success story, the spiritual character of the congregation was

deteriorating. He told me that the church had made it so easy for people to turn up, that they just switched off upon entering the worship. Attendees consumed the worship experience the way one would consume an hour-long TV program.

Such an attitude to worship is inconceivable when we consider the transcendent Christ of the book of Revelation. In chapter four of the book we are given an insight to heavenly worship:

> In the center, around the throne, were four living creatures, and they were covered with eyes, in front and in back. The first living creature was like a lion, the second was like an ox, the third had a face like a man, the fourth was like a flying eagle. Each of the four living creatures had six wings and was covered with eyes all around, even under its wings. Day and night they never stop saying:
>
> "'Holy, holy, holy is the Lord God Almighty,'
> Who was, and is, and is to come."

Whenever the living creatures give glory, honor, and thanks to Him who sits on the throne and who lives for ever and ever, the twenty-four elders fall down before Him who sits on the throne and worship Him who lives for ever and ever. They lay their crowns before the throne and say:

> "You are worthy, our Lord and God, to receive glory and honor and power, for you created all things, and by your will they were created and have their being."[8]

This scene of heavenly worship comes after the letters to the seven churches, linking earthly and heavenly worship. In chapter 1, Christ stands amongst the seven lamp stands, which represent the seven churches, a symbol of His direct presence and involvement within the churches. Such a viewpoint helps one to make sense of the old priest in the Lebanese valley's lonely worship service. Revelation reminds us that the witness and the worship of the Church are the "thin places" between heaven and earth. They are tastes of what life will be like when heaven and earth are reunited by God. The highly symbolic heavenly worship described in Revelation feels otherworldly. Yet despite its strangeness, it is a reminder that our attitudes here and now echo through eternity; that when we worship, pray, serve the poor, share the gospel, read the Word, these things matter in ways beyond just what we can experience through our senses. Such worship and discipleship flow out of an encounter with a transcendent God, and is the only thing that can chisel a road of devotion out of the stony terrain of secularism.

The radical thing about Abraham's encounter with God is that this transcendent, otherworldly God, who cannot be reduced to one location, who is unseen and holy, was to be worshipped in everyday life. When you compare the Bible to the scriptures of other religions, what is striking is the normality of the Bible. There are not gods or spiritual entities under every rock, or exhaustive descriptions of heavenly battles. Abraham is not taken away from the earth to another spiritual realm. God does speak to him, but the arena for his discipleship is the everyday. His relationship with the spiritual does not drive him away from everyday life, but instead pushes him deeper into it. The transcendent is to be found in the midst of the ordinary.

TWENTY-TWO:
FINDING TRANSCENDENCE IN THE ORDINARY

The growth of the macro and micro in our time has squeezed out the communal in our faith . . .

It is 6 AM and I have not slept. My head hurts and again there is a horrible taste in my mouth. This time, however, my exhaustion is not the exhaustion of travel, I have barely left my home in weeks. We have been up with the twins all night. My ears ring from the sound of their crying. I am changing a diaper, its odor hits me like a punch in the face. My wife is trying to say something to me but I cannot hear her due to the sound of crying. I turn to her to try to make out what she is saying. As I turn, the twin she is holding vomits all over her. We look at each other and shake our heads.

I HEAR A SMALL VOICE CRY OUT. IT IS MY THREE-YEAR-OLD DAUGHTER. "DADDY, WAKE UP! IT'S MORNING TIME!" I GROAN AND LOOK AT THE CLOCK.

This level of busyness and sleeplessness has been going on for weeks—and we are aware that this is just the beginning. Then just like that, the twins stop crying for the first time in hours and the possibility of sleep arises. We collapse into bed; I look at my clock. It is now 6:20. My exhausted body begins to finally relax and sleep begins to wash over me. Suddenly I am awakened. I hear a small voice cry out. It is my three-year-old daughter. "Daddy, wake up! It's morning time!" I groan and look at the clock. Six-forty. As I rise for the day and make my daughter breakfast I find my mind drifting back to the airports, the hotel rooms, the blue skies and white clouds outside of the airplane window. The road begins to whisper into my ear, "You don't have to be here."

At the heart of the mythology of the road is the desire to escape the mundane. The road genre pioneered by Kerouac has been criticized by a number of women as a form of male escapist fantasy, one characterized by stories of men who hit the road in order to run away from domestic responsibility. This escapist fantasy informs the culture of the road, fueling our fear of the mundane, the domestic, and the ordinary. The fantasy rekindles our pagan hearts and feeds our desires to transcend ourselves, to again mimic Babel, crossing the divide between human and god. God's answer to the sin of Babel was a single man, and a single family. It was not the religion of escapism but the practice of incarnation. The art of enfleshing His way in ordinary life. God's intention was never to aid us in our escape of this planet but rather to transform life here. The Sumerians built ziggurats to reach the gods. The religions of the Middle East worshipped their gods on mountains and high places. The God of Israel would be a God who walked alongside, who demanded worship in the everyday, the giving over of the whole of life to Him. God eventually would incarnate Himself amongst humanity—dying on a cross in the midst of the chaos and corruption of human life.

> THE ROAD BEGINS TO WHISPER INTO MY EAR, "YOU DON'T HAVE TO BE HERE."

REBUILDING OUR SENSE OF THE COMMUNAL

If Abraham were around today and we were advising him on his partnership with God in rebuilding the world, we would no doubt have countless suggestions for him in his quest. He would need to get the message out; we would get him on Twitter, set up a Facebook fan page for him. Cultural currency would be key, so building a profile and a "brand Abraham" would have to be a priority. A few gritty and well-shot pics of a brooding Abraham in some urban locales would add to his aura of authenticity. If we could get his stunning wife Sarah in the shot, and maybe some graffiti, or even better stencil art, in the background, we would be onto a winner. Maybe then we could create an event, not a conference, but a gathering in a non-typical location, like an abandoned factory or an old train station. Somewhere that gave the whole movement a sense of cool.

A book deal would be fantastic; a story filled with anecdotes, inside scoops, and the right amount of controversy would be killer. Some viral videos would push things along. An accompanying album featuring some up-and-coming Christian indie bands, with tracks inspired by the man, would be magic. Getting him on the speaking circuit at the big conferences would be essential. Of course whilst his Middle Eastern base adds a sense of mystery and brand differentiation, the travel times would be problematic. It would be much better if he could be persuaded to pack up and move to the United States. The ideal base would be somewhere in the Midwest, close to an airline hub with good access to the coasts. The goal would be to create a Seth Godin-esque tribe of fans. If we could do this we would really have something. No doubt Amazon rankings, media coverage, and interest would go through the roof. Success in our contemporary understanding would have seen Abraham excarnated from everyday life, "up in the air" floating above America in planes, on the speaking merry-go-round, divorced from everyday life. Always on the move, always on the road. Abraham would no longer be fleshing out faith in the everyday; he would be another Christian celebrity with a theory.

WE FILL BOOKS AND CONFERENCES WITH IDEAS AND THEORIES THAT ARE UNTESTED AND DISCONNECTED FROM REAL LIFE.

The words "theory" and "travel" are linked. The Greek word *theorin* was applied to a citizen of a Greek city who would travel to another city to observe a religious ceremony. *Theorin* is a detached viewing, just as the culture of the road is a detached approach to life, which is always ready to pick up and go when things get difficult. Despite our Christian faith, we often fall back into this detached approach. We fill books and conferences with ideas and theories that are untested and disconnected from real life. The religion that God was creating in Abraham was radical because it was to be lived out in the muck and mess of everyday life.

Abraham was part of a tribe, but it was nothing like the loose collection of half-committed fans, book consumers, and website visitors that contemporary marketers describe as tribes today. God promises to give Abraham a name; that he will be the father of multitudes, but Abraham will not walk the path of fame. The builders of Babel had attempted to create glory and fame by making a name for themselves in their own power. Abraham's path is one in which he will play an astonishing part in God's plan to rebuild the world, but this process will also be accompanied by God rebuilding him. The pagan virus within him must be killed, just as it must be killed in us. Abraham's mission will run parallel with his own reeducation in the ways of the one true God. The tribe in which Abraham lives, the collection of everyday relationships, will be the arena in which God will school and rebuild Abraham. Nothing has changed in our day, the arena of relationships and responsibility is the classroom in which God molds our character. How we respond to God's promptings and commandments is not just key to our own developments, but to the world. Yet the culture of the road has shrunk God's main classroom for teaching us His ways.

HOW OUR UNDERSTANDING OF COMMUNITY SHAPES OUR FAITH

For most of history and in many places around the world, most people have existed in a very similar situation to Abraham, spending their lives surrounded by a tribe, an extended family of committed relationships. The following image illustrates for us how humans have traditionally existed on a social level. We have found ourselves encased in three levels of connection. The broadest level is the Macro level:

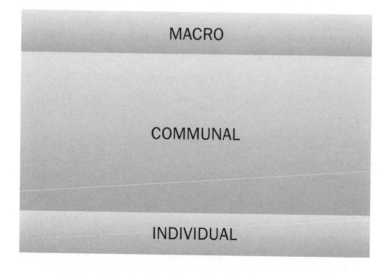

The Macro level is groupings of the largest scale. A grouping that would fit into the Macro could be an empire like the Roman,

Ottoman, or British Empires, a giant diverse collection of people. It could also be an ethnic or language group like the Chinese, Zulus, or Spanish speakers. The Macro level could also describe a nation. You don't really have to do much to be part of a Macro grouping; normally all you have to do is be born in a particular place, or into a particular ethnic group.

Following the Macro level is the Communal level. This grouping would describe clans, tribes, villages, small communities, of around four to two hundred hundred people. This is a grouping in which everyone knows you, not necessarily in depth, but at least they know your name and your face. Notice that in the diagram this level is the largest, this is the grouping that most people in history and on the planet now spend their time in. It is where they socialize, trade, and do their business. The lowest level is the Individual level. Here is the interior world of the individual, their inner life, their thoughts.

As the West developed and the industrial revolution caused people to move to the city, the connections and community found in villages began to fade. Cities grew rapidly, filling with rural people looking for work. The social fabric began to tear, crime and poverty became rampant. By the seventeenth century, the term post-Christian was being used to describe the city of London, as the communal space disappeared. Culture was forced to re-invent the communal space, and thus society was filled with all kinds of societies, clubs, salons, guilds, and organizations. Churches invested in community building, creating all kinds of communal spaces for dislocated city dwellers. This period saw people of faith give birth to the Salvation Army, the Sunday school movement, the Royal Society for the Prevention of Cruelty to Animals, and the YMCA. This was the era in which countless churches were planted, bringing a sense of community to formerly isolated neighborhoods and cities.

Even cafes were completely different from how we understand them today. Instead of just providing a caffeine hit, cafes were highly organized forums for social, political, or spiritual debate. Historians have noted the role discussions held in cafes, social clubs, and salons had in sparking the American and French revolutions. At one time the British government considered banning cafes, thus stopping citizens from freely exchanging information. Groups within the communal level are defined by volunteerism, participation, commitment—a sense of duty and service.

Since the rise of the culture of the road a constriction has occurred. The Macro level has expanded, cities have grown, the State's size has increased, some corporations are now bigger than medium-sized countries' economies. Universities have grown, some with campuses around the world. The Internet with its almost inconceivable size sits squarely within the Macro level. The Individual level has also significantly increased. The individual's expectations of life, the shift from social obligations to individual rights, the sheer expanse of choice, and the growth of radical individualism have all combined to expand the self, and the Individual level.

MACRO

COMMUNAL

INDIVIDUAL

The growth of the Macro and the Micro levels has squeezed out the Communal. The decline of the Church has been matched by the decline and reduction of the Communal level. The decline of church attendance in the West has mirrored the decline in participation of societies, guilds, unions, and lodges. It is estimated that during the nineteenth century in London, on any weeknight one in five adult males were out engaged in face-to-face relationships. Involved in societies, organizations or voluntary associations. Such figures are unimaginable in our world of screens.

The growth of the macro and micro in our time has created the possibility of an individualized faith that is almost totally detached from the communal, a faith built around books, podcasts, conferences, and a passive, anonymous consumption of worship. There is nothing wrong with books, blogs, and podcasts, nor is there anything wrong with large churches or big conferences. In their correct place they can be fantastic resources; but if they are the only avenue of spiritual growth, an unhealthy faith will develop. Community, accountability, and correction are fundamental to faith: without them our wills rather than Christ will dominate. Jean Vanier, who has written eloquently on the need for Christian community, wisely notes:

> Community . . . is the place where our limitations and our egoism are revealed to us . . . we discover our poverty and our weakness, our inability to get on with people, our mental and emotional blocks . . . our seemingly insatiable desires, our frustrations and jealousies, our hatred and our wish to destroy.

In the culture of the road our true broken selves are never revealed, because when things become difficult, when our hurts and pain are revealed, when individual wills are challenged, we physically or mentally move on. Abraham is forced by God to move deeper into the communal space, his sins and fears are revealed to him. The process is painful, yet God meets him there, Abraham grows into the father of the faith.

Living out one's faith can be difficult in cities, towns, or suburbs where the communal space has all but disappeared. The task for the believer, then, is not just to live out one's faith within the communal realm, but in a secular culture to rebuild it. At a college commencement speech, novelist Kurt Vonnegut Jr. told the assembled graduates that the most daring thing they could do with their youth would be "to create stable communities in which the terrible disease of loneliness can be cured." God's commandment to Adam and Eve was to go forth and multiply. God promised Abraham that he would be the father of a nation. There is no doubt that there is a biological imperative in these commandments and promises, but for you and me as God's *Shomer*, our mandate to cultivate creation, and to model Christ's reconciling love to us, is to rebuild the communal space through modeling covenantal love.

TWENTY-THREE:

THE RELATIONSHIP THAT CHANGES THE WORLD

Humans need covenant.
Without it we drown in our freedoms . . .

Kerouac and his friends the Beats attempted to reengineer the communal space. Kerouac's group of peers anticipated the rise of fluid social groupings, which some commentators have labeled urban tribes—collections of peers who hold a loose commitment that is based around the group pursuit of pleasure and experience, a pursuit that provides some relational solace but still allows the individual ultimate freedom. Douglas Coupland's seminal nineties novels[1] popularized the trend of the urban tribe. Network television quickly picked up this social shift. The families of the eighties sitcoms became the urban tribes of the nineties and thus the space was created for *Seinfeld, Friends, How I Met Your Mother*, and countless other popular shows featuring loose groupings. The main drama that runs through these programs is the tension and confusion that exists around relational commitment. Commitment is something to be feared. At the same time the protagonists realize that for a human life to mean something one must have relationships, thus the plots revolve around the quest to enjoy the solace that relationships bring, and yet to maintain maximum personal freedom.

In these programs, marriage in the immediate is to be feared. The decision to enter a lifelong commitment is seen as agonizing, one which carries with it the positive potential to bring happiness and self-actualization, or negatively to cause a sense of entrapment, a limiting of choices that would bring sadness and boredom. The possibility of children is even more feared and carries the potential to severely limit characters' ability to exercise their wills. Marriage and children are definitely portrayed as beneficial future possibilities, but, as in a game of chicken, the characters must hold out for these possibilities until the last possible moment.

The urban tribes and platonic groups of TV and real life fall well short of the covenantal. Near the end of *On the Road*, Dean (Neal) leaves a seriously ill Sal in Mexico for a woman. In his lowest moment, Sal is let down by the urban tribe he has created. Its bindings are not strong enough to rein in the will.

WHY OUR ATTACHMENTS ARE UNDER ASSAULT

Commentators have observed that the life of Abraham is a series of tests. One of the first tests that Abraham faces is the temptation to leave his barren wife for another. One can imagine Abraham lying in bed at night worrying over the continuation of his line. His mind no doubt would have entertained the possibility of leaving Sarah and taking another wife. As eligible younger women passed him, surely he would have entertained the question "what if?" Abraham chooses instead to stay with Sarah. It is noteworthy that throughout his life Abraham's relationships are tested. He is separated twice from his wife by powerful rulers, he must part ways with his nephew Lot, his marriage almost falls apart as he sleeps with Hagar, and his ultimate test will involve the potential sacrifice of his son Isaac.

Jewish commentators have noted that it is telling that after leaving Haran, it is Pharaoh and all the power of Egypt that tries to separate Abraham from Sarah. For the Jews Egypt, or *Mitzrayim*, symbolized not only the actual political state of Egypt but a worldview that was in complete opposition to the way of God. Egypt was a culture fixated by death. In contrast Israel revolved around a love of *chaim* (life). Egypt followed many gods, whereas Israel bowed only before the one true God. Egypt was known by its power and its pyramids, Israel would be known by its faithfulness to God's instructions.

The Jews would link the spirit of *Mitzrayim* to Babylon, and the early Christians would follow the line to Rome. This worldview, in opposition to God, would attempt to break the committed bond between Abraham and his wife. What was at stake was not just a marriage, but God's plan to redeem the world through Abraham's offspring. This is a crucial point: in the biblical worldview, commitment leads to fruitfulness. The powers that work against God's plan for the world will always undermine our commitments, always fill us with the fear of relational entrapment. The powers and principalities of this world deal in commitment phobia.

THE POST-COVENANTAL CULTURE

The same charge can be leveled against our culture today. We have noted that while our culture can be described as secular, it is still one in which belief exists. Large percentages of Western populations still subscribe to a belief in God, and many list themselves as Christian or adhere themselves loosely to various denominations. Yet an authentic engagement with faith is lacking. So an interesting angle from which to view our culture is to see it as post-covenantal. It is the covenantal element of Christian faith that grates most strongly against the spirit of the day. For example, one charge that is leveled against Christian faith is that it is anti-sex. This could not be further from the truth. The Bible has no problem with sex; the biblical book Song of Songs can easily be classed within the genre of erotic literature. Compared to a faith such as Buddhism, which labels all desire as leading to suffering, biblical faith is affirming of sex and sexual desire. Christian teaching insists that intercourse is positive, healthy, and holy when practiced within the field of marital covenant. The point

IT IS THE COVENANTAL ELEMENT OF CHRISTIAN FAITH THAT GRATES MOST STRONGLY AGAINST THE SPIRIT OF THE DAY.

of difference, then, between our culture and biblical faith is not so much over the issue of sex, but over covenant. The ideas of covenant and wholehearted commitment are anathema to the culture of the road, which is grounded in ideas of personal autonomy and radical individualism. They were also anathema to Abraham's world,

yet the concept of covenant would be key to God's redemption of the world. Genesis 17 reads:

> When Abram was ninety-nine years old, the Lord appeared to him and said, "I am God Almighty; walk before me faithfully and be blameless. Then I will make my covenant between me and you and will greatly increase your numbers." Abram fell face-down, and God said to him, "As for me, this is my covenant with you: You will be the father of many nations. No longer will you be called Abram; your name will be Abraham, for I have made you a father of many nations. I will make you very fruitful; I will make nations of you, and kings will come from you. I will establish my covenant as an everlasting covenant between me and you and your descendants after you for the generations to come, to be your God and the God of your descendants after you.[2]

Abraham will be educated by God in a different mode of being. God will enter into a covenantal mode with Abraham that will flow into his ancestors, and into all areas of life. Abraham will learn to model a covenantal relationship with God in contrast to the utilitarian approach of his neighbors to their gods. Abraham and Sarah's marriage will model a covenantalism that is in contrast to the sexual and marital models all around them. Abraham will learn to love his family covenantally, he will learn to practice hospitality to the outsider, welcoming them and offering them relationship in contrast to the violence and inhospitableness of the surrounding nations. Abraham's lessons in covenantal living will provide the framework for the building of the people of God. Abraham's ancestors will learn that biblical life is lived within a covenantal matrix. A way of living in complete contrast to the world. Israel will be defined as a nation called to show a covenantal approach to marriage, sexuality, family, the poor, the outsider, creation, and most importantly to God.

WHY MARRIAGE IS NOT ABOUT MAKING YOU HAPPY

Kerouac failed miserably in the covenantal stakes when it came to sex and marriage. Through his life we see an absolute romantic desire to settle down and marry a woman, yet he fails again and again at this task. It is particularly telling that his double mindedness with sexuality and women mirrored his double mindedness with God.

Rabbi Shmuley Boteach in his book *Renewal*[3] quotes the Talmud, which says that if a man does not marry by twenty-five he will destroy God's world. This is an extremely shocking statement in our culture, which delays marriage. In the United States the average age of marriage for males is now 28; in my home, Australia, it is 29. Marriage in our culture is either portrayed as a blissful Edenic experience or a mundane, restrictive prison. Thus we either hide from marriage or seek it out, only to be hugely disappointed when its true nature emerges. How on earth could a man destroy God's world by not marrying by twenty-five? The ego of the male needs to exist within covenant, otherwise it will go rogue. Philip Yancey notes that marriage is not a place to "fulfill our romantic and ego needs."[4] Instead Yancey reminds us it is "God's great tool for character formation." Our culture has re-imagined marriage as a conduit of self-actualization. The high divorce rate in the West reveals the way in which we expect marriage to deliver us self-actualization. Couples expect marriage to deliver a transcendent shot of meaning to their lives; when this does not occur, the marriage or the partner gets the blame rather than our overinflated expectations. The story of Abraham reminds us that marriage is the arena in which we are shaped and disciplined, where we learn to lay down our own agendas. Humans need covenant. Without it we drown in our freedoms.

FRIENDS WITH BENEFITS

What about single people? Well, there are three types of single people that I am aware of. The first kind are people who desperately desire to be married: they have not found the right person, or they may have had their spouse leave them or pass away. Many today, particularly women, find themselves in this position, and I have endless compassion for them. They are the unspoken victims of the communal and covenantal breaking down in our culture. Every society throughout history has had mechanisms which facilitate courtship and marriage, but in our post-covenantal culture the system has failed.

The second kind of single person is someone who has committed to a life of celibacy, who believes that they are led by God to lead a life of singleness. Although shocking to our contemporary culture, obsessed with hedonism and instant gratification, which cannot fathom that someone would want to forgo an erotic connection with another for a higher good, this approach is wholly biblical.

The third type of person runs from commitment, keeping all of their options open, trying to maximize their personal autonomy, outsourcing their sexual, emotional, and relational needs. Ultimately this third person is in a marriage with themselves. They are the ultimate expressions of the philosophy of the road.

For much of Christian history, religious orders provided a covenantal space for the single. Not too long ago I had lunch with a member of a religious order. It was interesting to contrast his language to many of my single friends, he often used the term "we" to describe his brothers, rather than the obligatory "me." As a group of single men committed to Christian celibacy, their order provided lifelong community, accountability, support, and covenantal relationships in the same way that marriage does.

Philip Rieff claims that our society is ultimately set up for what he calls the loosely connected duo.[5] The endgame for our post-covenantal culture, the culture of the road's coupling *par excellence*, is the loosely committed duo, or to use the odious jargon of our day, "friends with benefits." Their occasional romantic interactions provide just enough of a shot of relationality to stave off existential loneliness. They use each other as simply tools, hedonistic rest stops on the highway of selfishness. A recent article that I read in the lifestyle section of the newspaper advised readers who were considering becoming "friends with benefits" to set rules from the beginning, to make sure that they both do not get too emotionally involved, that for such a liaison to work it must be kept purely about the physical. The article was a staggeringly blatant "how to" guide to mutual commodification, objectification, and compartmentalization.

What seems to our culture through its sociological eyes as consensual, when viewed through the theological lens is exposed as pagan, the reduction of living, breathing humans into tools to be manipulated. We are back on top of the Mesopotamian ziggurat here, as the temple prostitutes copulate, except the god is not Moloch or Baal but ourselves. This form of sexual commodification is ultimately idolatry. Christian writer John F. Kavanaugh contrasts God's covenantal way of being with our Western culture's habit of commodification. Our culture rips things from the covenantal frame and turns them into commodities. Kavanaugh insists that taking a covenantal approach to life is a radical act today that Christians must engage in:

> In a culture which portrays life-commitment as impossible and undesirable, which inhibits the flowering of true intimacy, which deems a suffering love and sacrifice to be negative values, men and women who enter into a personal covenant by mature and free consent are taking a radical stance.[6]

Like Abraham, we must learn from marriage and family the ways of the covenantal mode. We must rebuild our world one small action at a time. Instead of escaping the commitments we find ourselves in we must reorient our perspective, re-envisioning those commitments as God's classrooms of spiritual formation. A Christian social researcher shared with me that his team's research had found that the more connected into a web of relationships, and the more altruistic your approach to life is, the more likely you are to attend church and have an active faith. Those who were married with children naturally did not just evaluate their lives through their own perspective, but were forced to think of the needs of their spouse and children, were far more likely to become engaged in spiritual community. Interestingly, single people, particularly women, who were engaged in people-centered vocations in which they served others such as social work and the health field, were also highly likely to be involved actively in church life. People whose outlook was primarily individualistic, who worked in fields which were highly competitive and primarily about financial gain, were far less likely to be involved actively in faith and church life. The least likely person to be seen in church was a single male, with a primarily individualist outlook on life, and who was pursuing materialist and financial goals.

CHOICE AND COVENANT

The covenantal approach understands that more attractive and appealing people than one's spouse will come across our paths; that people who are more fun, and more rewarding than our families, can always be found. That better options, better places than home, better careers can be sought out. That there will always be cooler, more exciting options than service, mercy, and mission. When we enter into the covenantal mode we hold no illusions that we will constantly be faced with opportunities to back out of our commitments. Thus we learn a key to biblical living, the practice of daily choosing to honor our commitments. Abraham's tests, the web of covenantal relationships in which he exists, force him to learn the art of daily choosing to honor his commitments. This approach is the backbone of faith, which at its heart is about choice and commitment. Kerouac attempted to live a life in which he chose faith, but a desire for freedom and autonomy dominated other parts of his life. The consequences were devastating, not just for him, but for those with whom he was in relationship. Abraham's life shows us that we cannot divorce the commitment and choice to follow God from our honoring of commitments in the other areas of our life. In our culture the practice and valuing of choosing to move toward commitment, to live a life of chastity, in a culture of sexual, social, and theological promiscuity, is not a prudish choice, it is as John Kavanaugh reminds us, an act of revolutionary resistance:

> Chastity, both in the marital and celibate forms, stands as a rare testimonial to human integrity, to the symbolic and actual importance of being embodied selves, to the pre-eminence of personhood and covenantal life. In a hedonistic culture, more-over, chastity is a most effective concrete critique of fulfillment through immediate gratification. It is a living refutation of the reduction of persons to either machines or animals, to prog-eny or pleasure. . . .This is why sexual integrity is under such relentless attack in advanced Western societies, why it has to be explained away as deviance, repression, or frustration. It is a scandal to Madison Avenue, Hollywood, and the halls of academe and Rockdom. . . .The life of married or celibate chastity can be a most subversive lived force today. It is truly counter-cultural.[7]

Kavanaugh's reflections help us understand the truly stagger-ing countercultural nature of another radical moment in the life of Abraham:

> Then God said to Abraham, "As for you, you must keep my covenant, you and your descendants after you for the genera-tions to come. This is my covenant with you and your descen-dants after you, the covenant you are to keep: Every male among you shall be circumcised. You are to undergo circumci-sion, and it will be the sign of the covenant between me and you. For the generations to come every male among you who is eight days old must be circumcised, including those born in your household or bought with money from a foreigner—those who are not your offspring. Whether born in your household or

bought with your money, they must be circumcised. My covenant in your flesh is to be an everlasting covenant."[8]

Circumcision is a powerful symbol, a pragmatic reminder of both human's propensity toward unfaithfulness and our need for covenant. The mark of circumcision was a dramatic break, a clear delineation between the emerging people of God and the surrounding nations. There is a wonderful pragmatism about the ritual, if Israel is to practice God's brand of love and justice, if it is going to walk to a new beat, it must do so at all levels of life. There will be no duality in God's new way between personal morality and social justice. This is as true today as it was in Abraham's time, God demands a whole of life faithfulness, no other kind of commitment is robust enough to withstand the powers and principalities which resist His work in the world.

God's covenant with Abraham blows out of the water our loosely held ideas of commitment today. This was not a Hollywood marriage with a detailed prenup, this was not a legal contract filled with fine print and get-out clauses. This was a blood and guts, determined, and passionate binding together. God would stand by Israel, a nation who would constantly let Him down, reject Him, and curse Him. God would stick to his commitment to Israel as his vehicle of salvation for humanity. God's dedication to this relationship would eventually see Him hanging on a Roman cross. This was not a relationship in which God could protect Himself; by entering into covenant with Abraham, God had everything to lose. It is this mode of being that we must rediscover. We must rebuild the shattered ruins of the covenantal in our culture. Sure, we can legislate change regarding the sanctity of marriage, we can launch media campaigns advocating for covenantal ways of living. The surest way, however, to revolutionize our world is to practice covenantality in our own lives.

TWENTY-FOUR:
CULTIVATING CREATION

Nature, understood in its context,
points us to Him who deserves worship . . .

The royalty of the culture of the road is the rock star. Nothing takes the culture further than the cliche of the rock star, always on tour, sleeping with groupies, dripping with fame and hedonism, always living in the moment. They are the high priests of the modern cathedral of transcendence—the concert. The term rock star is no longer used to just describe musicians but anyone in a particular field who has garnered a certain level of fame and who lives with rock star abandon. The term has even found its way into the Christian subculture, attaching itself to well-known writers and preachers. Such labeling creates the impression that there is a form of ministry or Christian life in which one can have the best that both faith and the road offer.

Mick Jagger of the Rolling Stones was not the first rock star, but he did more than anyone else to craft the image into what it is today. Jagger modeled his form of fame upon a group of English poets that were living a proto–rock star lifestyle in the north of England in the early nineteenth century. The group included

William Wordsworth, Percy Bysshe Shelley, and Samuel Taylor Coleridge. Frustrated as their society became more modern, and yet wary of orthodox Christian belief and scripture, the group turned to nature for a sense of wonder and transcendence. Laying the foundations for today's preference for individual spirituality over what is termed organized religion, the group came to believe that a life of meaning could be attained by an individual who sought transcendent, subjective experiences. Motivated by this new vision, the group created a kind of commune of like-minded intellectuals. They traveled, took drugs, and wrote poetry. Yet more than anything they were inspired by nature. The group lived together in the picturesque Lake District, a landscape composed of stunning lakes, hills, and rock formations. The poet standing alone, atop a breathtaking view, inspired by the sublime, was their ultimate means of experiencing the transcendent.

Yet there was a problem. Samuel Taylor Coleridge loved the moments of transcendence experienced at the face of a mountain, but he had to return to his unhappy marriage and domestic life. The individual, subjective moment of pleasure and awe in nature did not help one's sense of purpose of personal meaning when one was away from that moment. To maintain the buzz, Coleridge would take more and more drugs, while sinking into a depression. Eventually nature would no longer speak to him; it only intensified his pain. His poem "Ode to Dejection" would capture this sense of despondency: "A grief without a pang, void, dark, and drear, A stifled, drowsy, unimpassioned grief, Which finds no natural outlet, no relief, In word, or sigh, or tear."[1] Looking upon the sight of the moon rising over the lake, Coleridge grieves, "I see them all so excellently fair, I see, not feel, how beautiful they are!" His eyes can recognize the natural beauty of the scene he is viewing, but it no longer offers him a sense of the transcendent. Viewed in of itself it cannot speak to his soul. It is simply a disconnected experience, the breaking down of life into unrelated elements. Such a process, in the words of literary critic Aidan Day, "led to a vision of a universe that lacked any informing spirit, any vital principle of unity. The universe was an aggregate of dead parts, a universe of death."[2]

The culture of the road offers us pleasures and experiences, but they are disconnected, and ultimately they will leave us wanting. For creation to speak to us, to offer us transcendence, it must be understood in its God-given context.

EVERYTHING IN ITS RIGHT PLACE

It is telling that in Genesis 15 as God enters into His covenant with Abraham, He takes him outside and tells him to "look up at the heavens and count the stars—if indeed you can count them . . . So your offspring shall be." The purpose of this statement is twofold: Obviously this is a reaffirmation of God's promise that Abraham will be the father of a mighty nation, and that his descendants will be too numerous to count. However, I believe there is a second meaning to this act. God is reminding Abraham of his place, yes He is offering him an amazing place in history, a purpose and a promise, but He is also placing Abraham within context, reminding him of his limitations. By reminding Abraham that he cannot count the stars, God is stating that He is God and that Abraham is not. The heavenly vista reminds Abraham that he is not the creator, but rather a created being. The builders of Babel had become entranced by their grand tower, the city had taken the focus off of their mortality and limitations, thus preparing the ground for paganism and idolatry. This invitation to view the stars, however,

> **THE CULTURE OF THE ROAD OFFERS US PLEASURES AND EXPERIENCES, BUT THEY ARE DISCONNECTED, AND ULTIMATELY THEY WILL LEAVE US WANTING.**

reminds us that God's plan to redeem the world will be built upon a foundation of things being in the correct context.

Every morning I eat oats with honey and cinnamon for my first meal of the day. I would each morning grab from my spice rack the small container of cinnamon that I had purchased from the supermarket and sprinkle it across my food without a thought. Without realizing it I simply used the cinnamon as a reduced object. Then one day I picked up Giles Milton's book *Nathaniel's Nutmeg.*[3] The book tells the story of the spice trade, the lengths that European traders would go to acquire tiny amounts of spices from the other side of the world, from places such as Banda in Indonesia and the island of Zanzibar. I read how archeologists combing the very Mesopotamian deserts walked by Abraham have discovered in the ruins of a house dating to approximately 1721 BC a small vessel containing cloves. The shocking thing about this discovery is that cloves were only found in a handful of islands in the Indonesian archipelago. These cloves had been traded through countless hands, all the way across the ancient world to Mesopotamia.

I discovered that the Bible was filled with references to the alluring power of spices. Song of Songs used the imagery of the spices, the Magi heralded the arrival of Christ with the gift of spices, Joseph of Arimathea honored Christ by embalming His body in spices. I stopped buying my spices from the supermarket and began to venture into the local Indian and Arabic stores. I soon discovered the passion that these communities had for spices. They were not simply a substance to mindlessly toss onto my breakfast; they in the words of historian Jack Turner brought "a bulging bag of associations, myth and fantasy . . . a whole swathe of potent messages."[4] I began to learn about the various classic spice mixes, such as *garam masala* and *ras al-hanout*. Soon

I began to chat with the local Arabian store owner who would duck out the back, enthusiastically bringing out for me the latest stash of *Bahrahat* spice mix, prepared by a local chef and made from a secret family recipe. It was like I had been initiated into a secret society. Now my spice rack had transformed into a treasure chest—every time I opened my pantry a wave of spicy fragrances filled the kitchen with their aroma and my mind would be taken to stories, people, places around the globe by their scent. I had unwittingly de-commodified the world, no longer were spices simply items that I ripped from the supermarket shelf. They had been deepened, put in their proper place. By understanding their context and their story, their true worth had been revealed.

The scent of spices now fills me with gratitude; their aromas and tastes fill me with the wonder of God. Nature speaks, not as an experience in and of itself, something merely for the individual to consume, but understood in its context it points us toward Him who deserves worship. Psalm 19 reads:

> The heavens declare the glory of God;
> the skies proclaim the work of his hands.
> Day after day they pour forth speech;
> night after night they display knowledge.
> There is no speech or language
> where their voice is not heard.
> Their voice goes out into all the earth,
> their words to the ends of the world.[5]

Our role as God's *Shomer* in this time and place, which has forgotten God, which has atomized the world into broken pieces, is to help others understand the coherence of life and creation. To be interpreters for those who have lost the instructional manual. To place creation in its proper context.

WHY YOU ARE CALLED TO BE A COSMIC CHIROPRACTOR

Biblical faith does not divide the world into two competing camps, one evil, one good. Rather, its diagnosis concerns the valuing of elements of creation. Paganism and idolatry spring up when creation is disordered, when things are given the wrong value. Our world is like a mall in which burglars have broken in and mixed up all the price tags. Cartons of milk are worth thousands of dollars, and precious jewels only a few cents. G. K. Chesterton once observed:

> The modern world is not evil; in some ways the modern world is far too good. It is full of will and wasted virtues. . . it is not merely the vices that are let loose. The vices are, indeed, let loose, and they wander and do damage. But the virtues are let loose also; and the virtues wander more wildly, and the virtues do more terrible damage."[6]

According to biblical spirituality there is nothing wrong with sex, or with food, or with intimacy. There is nothing evil about our individuality, our desire for happiness or fun. However, a world that has displaced God looks to gain from these things more than they were ever intended for. Thus things that are good in their God-given place within creation become swollen, pressurized beyond their limits. The virtues go rogue. Chesterton complains, "The modern world is full of the old Christian virtues gone mad. The virtues have gone mad because they have been isolated from each other and are wandering alone."[7]

Creation makes sense, and represents the will of God when it is appreciated, understood, and held together as a whole. Secular culture, seeing no hand and no purpose behind the cosmos, shatters the coherence of the world. Think for example of food. Earlier we mentioned the mode of eating that grew up around the culture of the road. The flattened, reduced parody of food that is fast food. Fast food is not designed to provide nutrition, but to fulfill lusts for quick hits of sugar and fats. Its empty calories do not satisfy, it is not crafted to be a center-point of community life but is designed to be eaten in cars or on lonely plastic seats made specially to encourage patrons to keep moving.

Yet food in the biblical imagination is a gift from God, evidence of His care for us. Providing us with nutrition and energy, food is utterly vital to our health. Food is a binding element, bringing together families, communities, and the people of God. It is a conduit for community and for pleasure. Passover, communion, and the messianic feast at the end of the age all feature food. Scripture reminds us that moved out of its rightful place, food when overconsumed can become problematic. That gluttony is the evidence of food taken out of its God-ordained place. God's intention is to bring creation back into its ordered whole. Michael Goheen and Craig Bartholomew observe:

> God's work of renewal is, by his own spiritual power, to redirect that whole creation back to himself, to its healthy functioning, to its intended goal, and to its place in the creation order. Thus we can speak of the way that God designed language, sex, economic life, political authority, scholarship, sports, and so forth to function. All these have been adversely affected by the power of sin. All have been misdirected; none functions the way God intended. Yet God's reconciling work is aimed at countering this distorting power with a loving power: to redirect and renew all these things so that they may function as he had always intended for them.[8]

We are invited to join God in this task. Chesterton describes our world as something like a shipwreck, which we happen upon.

There are the broken planks of the hull, but there is also treasure to be found amongst the wreckage. Thus the role that God has for Abraham, and for us, is to partner with Him in repairing the world. To put things back in their right place, to pick the treasure from the debris, to repair the hull, to be cosmic chiropractors. Following God's commandments for living is not an exercise in moralism, nor is it an attempt to acquire salvation through works. Instead when we follow God's ways we place everything in its God-ordained place, we are fulfilling our roles as the *Shomer*.

LIVING A DIFFERENT STORY

God's story, His actions in history, is the narrative that gives life a sense of coherence. Abraham changed the world because he was invited by God to play a part in His grand story. A story which was in complete contrast to his pagan neighbors who believed that history was stuck in a constant loop, always repeating. Just like our culture of the road, one could never come to a conclusion or a resolution, the destination hovered perpetually over the horizon. Yet God's story was different, the world was broken, God was intervening and He would mend the world. God invited Abraham into His story in a unique way. After God invited Abraham to view the stars, He asks Abraham to engage in an even stranger action:

> So the Lord said to him, "Bring me a heifer, a goat and a ram, each three years old, along with a dove and a young pigeon." Abram brought all these to him, cut them in two and arranged the halves opposite each other; the birds, however, he did not cut in half. Then birds of prey came down on the carcasses, but Abram drove them away. As the sun was setting, Abram fell into a deep sleep, and a thick and dreadful darkness came over him. Then the Lord said to him, "Know for certain that for four hundred years your descendants will be strangers in a

*country not their own and that they will be enslaved and mis-
treated there. But I will punish the nation they serve as slaves,
and afterward they will come out with great possessions. You,
however, will go to your ancestors in peace and be buried at
a good old age. In the fourth generation your descendants
will come back here, for the sin of the Amorites has not yet
reached its full measure." When the sun had set and darkness
had fallen, a smoking firepot with a blazing torch appeared and
passed between the pieces.*[9]

The Protestant Reformer Martin Luther interpreted this passage as God giving Abraham a vision of the path of history that
would flow from His covenant. Luther saw the dismembered
birds as symbolic of the Israelites, who would suffer under the
Egyptians symbolized by the birds of prey who came to eat them.
The early rabbis saw the act as God revealing to Abraham His
whole plan of redemption for history. R. R. Reno notes that Jesus
Himself says, "Your father Abraham rejoiced that he was to see
my day: he saw it and was glad." At the very onset of the covenant
Abraham was given an insight into the context of God's intervention into the world. God's intervention would be all about context,
it would be a covenant that was enfleshed in history. In contrast
to people of the road who see themselves as free radicals floating
in a meaningless universe, unattached to anything, God's plan
would be one that was worked out in a world in which context and
relatedness mattered. In it nothing floated in isolation. His plan
was a narrative, with a beginning, a middle, and a conclusion.

We have attached ourselves to the narrative of the road
because it seemingly gives us a sense of meaning in our confusing world, this was Kerouac's contribution to our culture. Yet two
short years before Kerouac took off on his road trip that would
change the world, another man would have an experience, an

experience that he would also turn into a bestseller. Kerouac's life would turn tragic, just like this man's. Yet unlike Kerouac, this writer would find hope in the midst of tragedy. Unlike Kerouac who held loosely to faith until his last days, this man would wed himself to the road of faith, following his savior to the Cross. A writer who truly lived life as God's *Shomer*, when his world was turned into a living hell.

TWENTY-FIVE:
FINDING HOPE IN AN ATOMIC HOLOCAUST

Anyone who is attuned to God's hand in history knows that there is always a remnant...

A DEATH SENTENCE

Takashi Nagai[1] slowly walked home, wondering how to tell his wife Midori that he would soon be dead. His heart broke as he contemplated the three years that he would have left with his young son and daughter. Like so many medical scientists working in the early days of radiography, overexposure to radioactive materials had resulted in his succumbing to leukemia. As he walked past his fellow citizens of Nagasaki, Japan, Nagai could have never imagined that soon they would join him in his radioactive death sentence.

As Nagai walked he prayed. His newfound Christian faith gave him a sense of solace that his former atheism never could. The scientist had changed when he picked up *Pensées*, a Christian apologetic written by his fellow scientist and hero, seventeenth-century thinker Blaise Pascal. Pascal's book and the experience of watching his mother die had convinced Nagai that there was more to life than just what could be seen and measured. After his conversion, his faith had been cultivated and strengthened by a wise old Christian he had encountered. Nagai, so used to the world of academia, was shocked to discover that his mentor was a simple janitor. Most of the Christians of Nagasaki held menial jobs, their faith pushing them to the margins of society.

By marrying Midori, Nagai married into a family descended from Japan's "hidden Christians." Although possible evidence is emerging of an earlier arrival, Christianity arrived in Japan in the sixteenth century, growing steadily until the government began a systematic and violent persecution against Japanese believers. This persecution resulted in many Christians settling in the Nagasaki area, in particular the suburb of Urakami. The government, fearing the Christians would align themselves with foreign powers, decided to intimidate the Christian population of Nagasaki by crucifying twenty-six Christians. One of the crucified, Paul Miki, preached to the watching crowd from his cross. As the early church father, Tertullian, noted, the blood of the martyrs spurs on the growth of the Church. This growth would see an intensification of violence that rivaled or even outdid the persecution of the early Church. Many Christians were forced to stand on an image of Christ. Those who did were freed; those who refused were subjected to the most unimaginable deaths. Thousands were crucified, others' bodies broken over wheels, some were sawn into pieces, others thrown into hot lava or boiling springs. The worst death was considered the upside down hanging in which the victim was hung upside down over a pit of excrement until death. For Japanese Christians at this time, Jesus' encouragement to take up one's cross was a literal rather than figurative commandment.

The Japanese Church remained underground for centuries

> FOR JAPANESE CHRISTIANS AT THIS TIME, JESUS' ENCOURAGEMENT TO TAKE UP ONE'S CROSS WAS A LITERAL RATHER THAN FIGURATIVE COMMANDMENT.

until international pressure for religious freedom began to mount. The Civil War general Ulysses S. Grant was a strong advocate of the freedom of the Japanese Christians. His pressure led directly to the building of Urakami Cathedral, which would become more than just a church for the Christians of Nagasaki. The chosen site for the church was the land on which Christians were forced to trample on the image of Christ. The church would become a symbol of the martyrs of Japan's faith in the face of death.

During World War II the Christians of Nagasaki would face more persecution. Government officials, believing that their faith would make them possible double agents, sent secret police to harass and intimidate them. The persecution seemed like a return to the old days—however, a far worse fate was in store for the Christians of Nagasaki.

The city was not intended to be the original target of an atomic attack. Instead, the bomb that was dropped on Nagasaki was intended for the town of Kokura. But poor visibility over Kokura led the bombing crew to the secondary target of Nagasaki. The crew used the steeple of Urakami Cathedral to guide their bombing run. The Christians of Nagasaki, so used to suffering, would experience another crucifixion, as a weapon of unimaginable power would flatten their homes.

Kerouac and his friends had talked about the spiritual and psychic effects of the atomic attack upon Japan, and the way that the bomb had altered the mind-set of the West. For Dr. Nagai, the atomic attack would not be an intellectual metaphor, or an abstract sociological phenomenon; it would be his chance to follow his Savior to the cross.

It is almost impossible to imagine the horror that the citizens of Nagasaki experienced at the dropping of the bomb. At first the flash of light, passing through walls, cars, people, anything. Then the wind, the force of the explosion, erasing a city in a second. There are two aerial images of Nagasaki that you can find easily online. The before shot shows an orderly city with streets and buildings. The second shot, taken after the blast, could be of an empty plain or a desert. Yet the damage to buildings was nothing compared to the violence the blast would inflict on men, women, and children. The fortunate ones were turned to ash in a second. Those within a few miles of the blast were skinned alive. Many victims, surveying the destruction, doubted their own sanity, so horrendous was the carnage. One young woman recalled looking out of her window seconds after the blast. Gone were the houses and buildings, the trees, the grass. All around her were skinned people and mangled bodies. She began to believe that she had literally been transported to hell.

Historians have debated the ethics of the atomic attacks upon Japan. Some argue that the death toll was a terrible necessity; that an invasion of Japan could have seen over a million deaths. Others will note that more people were killed in the bombing of the German city of Dresden with conventional weapons. Yet when we move beyond trying to hypothesize over civilian deaths, when we look to the bomb as the bitter fruit of humanity rather than any nation in particular, when we examine the bomb through biblical eyes, a terrible reality emerges. If humankind in Eden was charged with the role of *Shomer*, to worship God, to live in peace with other humans, to care for and cultivate creation, the atomic attacks upon Japan were a complete rejection of God's call upon humanity. God had breathed life into dust and created Adam; the bomb had breathed its horrible wind and turned humans back into lumps of ash. God had created the world out of the formless earth, the bomb turned a living, breathing city, an ecosystem, back into a sick, formless earth.

THE DESTROYER OF WORLDS

As he completed the first successful test of the first nuclear bomb in 1945, scientist Robert Oppenheimer quoted the Hindu scriptures: "Now I am become death...death...death, the destroyer of worlds."[2] Humankind had taken our role as *Shomer* and thrown it back in God's face. Yet anyone who reads Scripture, who is attuned to God's hand in history, knows that there is always a remnant. It is precisely at the moment when hell appears to win that resurrection becomes possible. Amongst the rubble and ruins, amongst the burning flesh and dead earth, amongst the horror and chaos, a man dying of cancer would take up the role of God's *Shomer*.

Bleeding from the head, covered in wounds, his hospital in flames, Takashi Nagai worked feverishly to save bedridden patients. As he pulled people from the flames, he worried about his wife. At least he knew that his children were safe, visiting a relative in the countryside. Every fiber in his being must have wished to go and find his wife, yet the staff of the university hospital needed a leader; people needed saving. God raises strange leaders in strange times, and a mantle of leadership would be placed upon Nagai's shoulders at that moment, a mantle and an authority that would only grow.

The military doctors arrived, and Nagai, after saving countless lives, was able to look for his wife. He picked his way through his flattened neighborhood. Urakami Cathedral was burnt to the ground. Eventually he found his home. In the kitchen was a lump of bones and ash. It was the remains of his wife, Midori. In the days after his terminal cancer diagnosis, Nagai had imagined his death. He had found solace in the knowledge that his last moments would be spent holding his praying wife's hand. Yet here was the woman he loved, turned back into dust. How could he have known that it would be she who would die first, that he would find himself squatting as black rain fell from the sky, shoveling his wife's remains into an old bucket? Then he saw it—in the bones of Midori's hand, her cross. Nagai broke down. It was the only thing which made sense in a world gone mad, the only thing which could bring life into the valley of death.

LIVING A THEOLOGY OF THE CROSS

Exhausted and overcome by his injuries, it looked as if Nagai would join his wife in death. As he lay sick, Nagai would think of Maximilian Kolbe. As a new Christian, Nagai had met the Polish priest, who had established a monastery outside of Nagasaki. Upon his return to Europe, Kolbe's protection of his Jewish neighbors saw him sent to the Auschwitz concentration camp. After an escape attempt had been made, the camp commander chose ten random men to die as a warning to the other prisoners. When one of the men cried out for his wife and children, Kolbe offered his life instead. The men were left in a hole to starve to death. Kolbe prayed for the men, ministering to each of them as they died. Kolbe was the last to die, with the guards injecting him with poison.

In the midst of the hell of the Holocaust, Kolbe lived out his sacrificial Christian faith. As he made an incredible recovery, Nagai made the decision to do the same, to give his final three years for his children, to rebuild his community, and to live as Christ's servant amongst the ruins.

As Nagai went about the business of caring for the victims of the bombing, his mind was filled with questions. Why Nagasaki and not Kokura, the original target? Why did the Christians of Nagasaki after centuries of persecution suffer so badly again? Eventually after much prayer, and reflection upon the Cross,

Nagai would come to a stunning conclusion. Amongst the ruins of Urakami, the Christians of Nagasaki would hold an open-air-remembrance service. Such was Nagai's growing stature that he was asked to speak. Before the hushed assembled crowd, he shared his belief that God had chosen for the bomb to fall upon the Christians of Nagasaki. Not because they deserved punishment, but because centuries of identification with Christ in His suffering had prepared them for what was to come. The Christians of Nagasaki had been chosen to give their lives so that the world might see the effects of atomic war, and never again use this weapon of mass destruction. Some members of the crowd in anger at his words stood to their feet and attempted to shout him down, but Nagai continued. Only a life lived in the shadow of the Cross could bring hope. Nagai would preach to the crowd:

ONLY A LIFE LIVED IN THE SHADOW OF THE CROSS COULD BRING HOPE.

> Happy are those who weep; they shall be comforted. We must walk the way of reparation . . . ridiculed, whipped, punished for our crimes, sweaty and bloody. But we can turn our minds' eyes to Jesus carrying his Cross up the hill of Calvary. . . . The Lord has given; the Lord has taken away. Blessed be the name of the Lord.

The Christians of Nagasaki had been given the opportunity to walk in the footsteps of Jesus toward the Cross, Nagai's life amongst the ruins would be a living testament to this belief. Despite his own illness and injuries, Nagai would continue to care for the sick and dying of Nagasaki. He would write a book studying the effects of radiation poisoning, offering his own body for research. Nagai at every opportunity would share his faith in Christ with the victims of the bombing. One young man who appeared at Nagai's door began to scream at the doctor, venting all of his frustrations and anger at the bombing. Nagai sat, patiently waiting until the man finished, and then quietly shared his faith, leading the man to Christ. A small group of men began to surround him, men whom he would disciple, who would become his arms and legs as his body failed.

THE BELLS OF GOD

Nagai understood the power of symbols, especially in times of disaster. One day he and his disciples made their way to the ruins of Urakami Cathedral. They discovered that despite the church being destroyed, the church bell was, incredibly, intact. The men created an improvised frame, and at dawn began to ring the bell. Its sound boomed out across Nagasaki, echoing around the debris. For the victims of the bombing, waking to another day in the lunar landscape that was once their city, the poignancy of the moment was almost overwhelming. I imagine Nagai and his friends, wretched in rags, bodies filled with radioactive poison, with all of their might ringing the heavy bell. Each peal going out over the landscape the way God's word moved over the formless earth at the beginning of the world. Each peal breathing life into dead minds, dead hearts, and dead earth. Each peal a reminder that after the crucifixion comes the resurrection.

A SMALL GROUP OF MEN BEGAN TO SURROUND HIM, MEN WHOM HE WOULD DISCIPLE, WHO WOULD BECOME HIS ARMS AND LEGS AS HIS BODY FAILED.

Each peal a reminder that in a landscape of hell, heaven can be heard. The moment was transformative for Nagai; it was a living testament to the fact that Christ was more powerful than the atomic age.

The moment would form the motif for Nagai's book *The Bells of Nagasaki*. Despite Japan's suspicion of Christianity, the book became a bestseller. Eventually the book was turned into a top-grossing movie. As the world reeled from the scale of the destruction of the atomic attacks upon Japan, and from the revelations of the full horrors of the Nazi Holocaust, Nagai's book would resonate with a world in search of meaning. Money from royalties began to pour in. Nagai now had the means to move away from Nagasaki, to seek medical help elsewhere, his fame ensuring that an escape from the broken city was possible. The lure of the road beckoned. Yet Nagai took a different path. His friends built a small, humble hut for him amongst the wreckage. He would stay and give his life for his home, the way that Christ had given His life for the world.

As his body ailed, Nagai devoted his time to writing, prayer, and taking visitors, sharing with each the simple love of Christ and His message of hope. The trickle of visitors turned into a torrent, as ordinary Japanese people, Buddhist monks, Shinto priests, atheists, and agnostics came to this dying man in a simple hut, each looking for answers. Nagai would be visited by luminaries such as Helen Keller and famous musicians. Even the Pope would send an emissary.

Then the unthinkable. The man considered a demigod by his people, the Emperor of Japan, traveled to Nagasaki. The man whose face ordinary citizens could not even look at came to visit Nagai.

INTO YOUR HANDS . . .

Nagai made his final journey through the cold, quiet, early morning streets of Urakami. Nearing death, a stretcher was brought to take him to the hospital. The men whom he had led to Christ, whom he had taught to live out Christ's beatitudes in the radioactive glow of Nagasaki, carried him through the streets. Past the ruins of Urakami Cathedral, past the places where thousands were incinerated in the flash of an eye, past the survivors now rousing in the early morning light. At one point Nagai would ask his friends to stop so that they could pray for peace to break out in Korea, as war was erupting in the peninsula across the sea. Takashi Nagai would die, surrounded by his family, the men whom he had led to Christ, and the hospital staff he had trained to save lives. As he came to the moment of death, his crying son passed him the family cross that had hung on the wall. Nagai fixed his eyes upon the cross and quoted Jesus' words on the cross: "Father, into Your hands I commend my spirit." According to his wishes his body was made available to his students to study the effects of radiation poisoning, in the hope that their research could help the victims of atomic weapons. It was his last selfless act.

Twenty thousand people would attend Nagai's funeral. At the apex of the service, the man who had come to Nagai filled with rage yet who went away filled with Christ rang out the bell of Urakami Cathedral. It echoed across the city, a testament to a life lived in Christ. Nagai was buried next to Midori. Upon his grave was etched a verse from Luke's gospel, chosen personally by Nagai,

"We are unworthy servants; we have only done our duty."[3]

WE ARE ALIVE!

It takes a servant heart to see the world through God's eyes. Takashi Nagai, wracked with a terminal illness, living in a city of death, was able to see the world for what it is. His ability to view life through the prism of the Cross lives on as a testimony to us. One night, as families huddled together warming themselves around fires, in the ruins of what used to be their homes, Nagai awoke, and in the stillness listened to the sound of his small children breathing. Having walked the tightrope between death and life, the passing of this world and the kingdom to come, knowing that his time would soon be up, Nagai would write in his journal with barely contained happiness, "We're alive, we're alive! And a whole new day is waiting for us!" The joy that defies human understanding, the sense of transcendence, meaning, and purpose, is found by a man who when measured by the standards of our world has nothing. He lives in a shanty, his wife and friends are dead, he has few or no possessions, he will soon die, and he is immobile in a city blown apart by an atomic weapon. Yet the great paradox which infuses life and the cosmos is that he who gives his life for Christ gains the world, he who is a prisoner of God finds freedom. He who cries shall find joy.

> WE DO NOT NEED TO INFECT THE WORLD WITH A GENERATION OF BELIEVERS WHO ARE HIP AND COOL; WE NEED A CHURCH.

WHICH ROAD?

The choice before us is now clear. To follow our culture's collection of stories that go nowhere, to believe that the world is a meaningless place, out of which we can only hope to eke out passing moments of pleasure. To follow a road which at the end of our lives will leave us only with a well-groomed Facebook page, a collection of digital photos, and a library of downloadable songs and movies. Our lives will be reduced to a digital memorial that can be erased with the click of a mouse. We will live and die as shallow people living in a shallow culture.

The need of the hour is not for a church that is relevant. We do not need to infect the world with a generation of believers who are hip and cool; we need a Church, and we need believers who are deep. I wholeheartedly reject the dogma and opinions of the new atheists, but one comment I heard recently from author and atheist Stephen Fry stung. Commenting on contemporary Christianity,

Fry said, "God once had Bach and Michelangelo on his side, he had Mozart, and now who does he have? People . . . who reduce the glories of theology to a kind of sharing."[4] Fry's assessment is painful because it is true. The depth, breadth, and creation-changing mandate of Christianity has been squashed into a private religious experience, to be hidden away from the world. A truth robbed of force, reduced into a mere feeling. President of the Barna group David Kinnaman believes that it is precisely this reduced form of Christianity that is causing young adults to leave the Church in droves. Kinnaman writes:

> The faith too many of them have inherited is a lifeless shadow of historic Christianity, which insists that following Jesus is a way of life, not a laundry list of vague beliefs that have little meaning for how we spend our lives. I think the next generation's disconnection stems ultimately from the failure of the church to impart Christianity as a comprehensive way of understanding reality and living fully in today's culture. To many young people who grew up in Christian churches, Christianity seems boring, irrelevant, sidelined from the real issues people face. It seems shallow.[5]

The second choice before us is to, like Takashi Nagai, immerse ourselves in the story of a God who came to earth to die for the world. A God who calls us to follow a different road, a road which is tough, a road which does not always let us get what we want, a road of sacrifice and pain, a road that ends with a Cross. A Cross which opens our eyes to the true nature of reality. A Cross which enables us to see that the world is luminously alive. That it pulsates with the sacred, that each atom, every creature, bears the fingerprints of its creator. A place where in the poetic words of William Blake we can "see a world in a grain of sand, And a heaven in a wild flower—Hold infinity in the palm of your hand, And eternity in an hour.[6] Then we will be deep people, on a mission to deepen the world, reservoirs of living water in the secular desert, revealing the glory of God.

CONCLUSION: THE ROAD HOME

I am mic'ed up and ready to preach at a five-year-old church known as Trinity Grace, spread across various locations across New York City. Space is at a premium in Manhattan, and the Chelsea congregation meets in an old German Lutheran church. The church is only a short walk from Kerouac's and the Beats' old stomping ground in Greenwich Village. As I wait for the congregation to arrive, I walk around the worship space, imagining the toil and hard cash of the German immigrants who built this church as a sign of their devotion to Christ in a new land. The church had ministered to the needs of its community in Manhattan for over a century. As Germany plunged into chaos and the Nazi nightmare, the church would become a spiritual base for the tens of thousands fleeing the troubles in their homeland. The church would host members of the Confessing Church, those pastors who resisted Hitler's regime, well-known names such as Martin Niemöller and Helmut Thielicke. As I explored the building, I lamented the loss of the old world, when the Church was far from perfect, but commitment and devotion were still essential building blocks of faith. The church feels like the memorial, a museum, a sacred residue as the secular city grows in power around it.

Over the next twenty minutes the hall begins to fill with mostly young adults. Eventually the room is packed. As worship starts I notice something that at first I couldn't put my finger on. Something almost undefinable. At first I notice an absence. It is the absence of the looks of detachment and boredom. The absence of crossed arms, darting eyes, mouths chewing gum. There is an intensity to the worship, not in the cliched sense. Rather the singing seems more akin to a cry for survival, a deeply expressed desire to feel God in a city that is covered in the dust of Babel.

Halfway through my sermon I become aware of a silence in the room, a silence that has form and weight. A silence of openness, of receptivity to the Word. This is the silence that Kerouac waited for, the soundlessness of a restless culture brought silent by the Word. Then I begin to discern it. It hangs palpably in the air like a cloud. Unseen but felt. At some deep metaphysical level, those thousands of tiny choices have counted, choices for community over individualism, for covenant over consumerism, for Christ over self. The choices mingle, like elements uniting into a form. I recognize what I am sensing. It is not lost, it does not lie dormant in the stone of the church walls. It is still alive, it is here, in this room. A foundation of faith lost in a commitment-phobic culture. It is devotion.

HALFWAY THROUGH MY SERMON I BECOME AWARE OF A SILENCE IN THE ROOM, A SILENCE THAT HAS FORM AND WEIGHT. A SILENCE OF OPENNESS, OF RECEPTIVITY TO THE WORD.

Later that night I stand at the river and overlook Manhattan just as Kerouac had done over half a century earlier at the end of *On the Road.* Kerouac had thought of "all that raw land that rolls in one unbelievable huge bulge over to the West Coast, and all that road going, and all the people dreaming in the immensity of it." The dead America, wrought impotent and lifeless by contemporary life, flattened and objectified by secularism—that dead America is imagined blessed and reanimated by Kerouac as night falls. "The evening star must be drooping and shedding her sparkler dims on the prairie, which is just before the coming of complete night that blesses the earth, darkens all the rivers, cups the peaks and folds the final shore in." As the lights in a thousand rooms, in a thousand buildings, come on like artificial stars, I too think of the immensity of America. I close my eyes and think of a road leading out of the old German church in Chelsea, weaving in and out of the skyscrapers, through the cities, the plains and towns of America. Blessing the land and the continent all the way to the West Coast. Not pausing at the Golden Gate Bridge, but moving across the Pacific to my home, bringing redemptive words to the songlines and streets of my country, so beautiful and yet so lost. I think of the road leading through the cobblestoned streets of Copenhagen, winding around the buildings built on the scorched earth of Nagasaki. A road of healing, a road of generosity, a road of sacrifice. A road that fills a flattened, secular world with the mystery of God's breath. A road made for a trillion Abrahamic steps of faith. A road for servant feet covered in Golgothan dust. I think of a road paved with devotion to Christ, flowing out across the globe like veins, blessing the world.

I open my eyes and think of Jack Kerouac. I think of Jack Kerouac no longer haggard and forlorn, lost on the road, but now truly home. I think of Jack Kerouac.

ACKNOWLEDGMENTS

Firstly, I want to thank my wife Trudi. Writing a book with new-born twins is a challenge, not just for the writer but for his wife. Trudi was incredible; I could not have done it without her support and prayer. Thanks to all the people who supported us, especially in practical ways, those who cooked, brought meals, babysat and helped out, my parents Garry and Joy Sayers, my mother-in-law Hazel Rice, the wonderful people of Red Church who rallied behind us. Thanks to Ben Catford and Pete Evans who prayed faithfully and constantly for me during the writing. Thanks to Sarah Deutscher, Amy Stephenson, Glen Sayers, and Andrew Shamy, who read the manuscript as it was developing and offered advice. Thanks to Matt Deutscher for his wonderful cover. Thanks to Jess Hammond for the initial prompt to write a book on Kerouac. Thanks to Alan Hirsch for his advice and support. Thanks to Randall Payleitner, Duane Sherman, Madison Trammel, Brittany Biggs, and the team at Moody for believing in this book. Most importantly thanks to God, who constantly teaches me strength in weakness.

NOTES

Chapter 1: A Tale of Two Roads

1. "A Careful Sequence of Mundane Dealing Sows a Day of Bloody Terror for Hijackers." *Wall Street Journal*, October 16, 2001. http://interactive.wsj.com/articles/SB1003180286455952120.htm.

2. "Cracking the Terror Code." *Newsweek*, October 14, 2001. http://www.newsweek.com/2001/10/14/cracking-the-terror-code.html.

3. "Terrorists Partied with Hooker at Hub-area Hotel." *Boston Herald*, October 10, 2001. http://web.archive.org/web/20011010224657/http://www.bostonherald.com/attack/investigation/ausprob10102001.htm.

4. See original FBI documents at http://www.historycommons.org/source-documents/2001/pdfs/fbi911timeline106-210.pdf.

Chapter 2: How Worship Became Entertainment

1. Robert S. Ellwood, *1950: Crossroads of American Religious Life* (Lexington, KY: John Knox, 2000), 21.

2. Cited in "Sayyid Qutb's America." *NPR*, May 6, 2003. http://www.npr.org/templates/story/story.php?storyid=1253796.

3. http://www.scribd.com/Syed-QutbThe-America-I-Have-Seen/d/6412907.

4. Jack Kerouac, *The Dharma Bums* (New York: Penguin, 1976), 97.

5. Ibid.

6. "Is This the Man Who Inspired Bin Laden?" *The Guardian*, November 1, 2001. http://www.guardian.co.uk/world/2001/nov/01/afghanistan.terrorism3.

7. http://www.scribd.com/Syed-QutubThe-America-I-Have-Seen/d/6412907.

8. Ibid.

9. Psychologist Abraham Maslow had coined the term Self Actualization in his highly influential paper "A Theory of Human Motivation" in the journal *Psychological Review* in 1943, only a few years before Qutb's arrival in America. Maslow's concept would have a tremendous influence on the West's view of self in the coming decades.

10. D. Elton Trueblood, *The Predicament of Modern Man* (New York: Harper and Brothers, 1944), 104.

11. Hubert Dreyfus and Sean Dorrance Kelly, *All Things Shining: Reading the Western Classics to Find Meaning in a Secular Age* (New York: Free Press, 2011), Kindle Edition.

12. Wade Clark Roof cited in Nancy Pearcey, *Total Truth: Liberating Christianity from Its Cultural Captivity* (Wheaton, IL: Crossway Books, 2008), Kindle Edition.

13. Shmuley Boteach, *Renewal: A Guide to the Values-Filled Life* (New York: Basic Books, 2010), Kindle Edition.

Chapter 3: From Home to the Road

1. The discerning reader should be made aware that *On the Road* contains strong adult content, and it would be wise to approach it with appropriate caution. Neither the publisher nor the author endorse the book.

2. William S. Burroughs quoted in "America's king of the road." *The Observer*, August 5, 2007. http://www.guardian.co.uk/books/2007/aug/05/fiction.jackkerouac.

3. Thomas L. Friedman, *The Lexus and the Olive Tree: Understanding Globalization* (New York: Anchor Books, 2000), 31.

4. Hari Kunzru cited in "America's first king of the road." *The Observer*, August 5, 2007. http://www.guardian.co.uk/books/2007/aug/05/fiction.jackkerouac.

5. James K. A. Smith, *Desiring the Kingdom: Worship, Worldview, and Cultural Formation* (Grand Rapids, MI: Baker, 2009), 25.

6. See Daniel Harris, *Cute, Quaint, Hungry and Romantic: The Aesthetics of Consumerism* (New York: Basic Books, 200).

7. See Eric Schlosser, *Fast Food Nation: The Dark Side of the All-American Meal* (New York: Houghton Mifflin, 2001).

8. See http://www.crystalcathedral.org/about/history.php.

9. "The Pancake People, or, 'The gods are pounding my head.' *Edge,* March 8, 2005. http://www.edge.org/3rd_culture/foreman05/foreman05_index. html.

10. See Nicholas Carr, *The Shallows: What the Internet Is Doing to Our Brains* (New York: W. W. Norton, 2010).

11. "Breaking the Mold." *Leadership Journal,* June 13, 2011. http://www. christianitytoday.com/le/2011/spring/breakingmold.html. Make sure that you check out Jon's book written with Darren Whitehead, it's a must read. See Darren Whitehead and Jon Tyson, *Rumors of God: Experience the Kind of Faith You've Only Heard About* (Nashville: Thomas Nelson, 2011).

Chapter 4: The Journey

1. Cited in "Travels with Myself." *The Age*, January 17, 2010. http://www. theage.com.au/national/travels-with-myself-20100116-mdji.html

2. See Alain de Botton, *The Art of Travel* (New York: Vintage, 2004).

3. Graham Cray, Sylvia Collins-Mayo, Bob Mayo, and Sara Savage, *Making Sense of Generation Y: The World View of 15-25-Year-Olds* (London: Church House Publishing, 2006), 37.

4. See Steven Bouma-Prediger and Brian J. Walsh, *Beyond Homelessness: Christian Faith in a Culture of Displacement* (Grand Rapids: MI, Eerdmans, 2008).

Chapter 5: The Secular World

1. http://www.scribd.com/Syed-QutubThe-America-I-Have-Seen/d/6412907.

2. Ibid.

3. Lawrence Wright, *The Looming Tower: Al-Qaeda and the Road to 9/11* (London: Penguin, 2006), 23.

4. John Leland, *Why Kerouac Matters; The Lessons of On the Road (They're Not What You Think)* (New York: Viking Press, 2007), 153.

5. Robert Inchausti, *Subversive Orthodoxy: Outlaws, Revolutionaries and Other Christians in Disguise* (Grand Rapids, MI: Brazos, 2005), 60–70.

6. Ann Charters, *Kerouac: A Biography* (London: Picador, 1973), 58.

7. Jack Kerouac, *Windblown World: The Journals of Jack Kerouac 1947-1954* (New York: Penguin, 2004), 142.

8. Ibid.

Chapter 6: An Immanent World

1. You can see how such a mind-set meant that it was dangerous to be Jewish, Roma (Gypsy), or any other religious or cultural minority that could be seen as compromising the spiritual health of Europe.

2. Jack Kerouac, ed. Ann Charters, *Kerouac: Selected Letters 1940-1956* (New York: Viking, 1995), 285.

3. Ibid.

4. Ibid.

5. Charles Taylor, *A Secular Age* (Cambridge, MA: Harvard University Press, 2007), 542.

6. Michael Allen Gillespie, *The Theological Origins of Modernity* (Chicago: University of Chicago Press, 2008), Kindle Edition.

7. Terrence L. Nichols. *The Sacred Cosmos: Christian Faith and the Challenge of Naturalism* (Grand Rapids, MI: Brazos, 2003), 9.

8. Frederick L. Nussbaum, *The Triumph of Science and Reason 1660-1685* (New York: Harper & Row, 1953), 7.

9. Nichols, *The Sacred Cosmos*, 10.

10. Craig M. Gay, *The Way of the (Modern) World: Or, Why It's Tempting to Live As If God Doesn't Exist* (Grand Rapids, MI: Eerdmans, 1998), 22.

Chapter 7: Carving Out a Life of Meaning

1. Christian Smith and Melinda Lundquist Denton, *Soul Searching: The Religious and Spiritual Lives of American Teenagers* (New York: Oxford University Press, 2005), 157.

2. Will and Ariel Durant, *The Story of Civilization, Volume 4: The Age of Voltaire* (New York: Simon and Schuster, 1965), 123.

3. See Italian mummy source of 'the scream'? *Discovery News,* September 7, 2004. http://web.archive.org/web/20041011032521/http://dsc.discovery.com/news/briefs/20040906/scream.html.

4. "Munch's agonising masterpiece." BBC Online News, Sunday, August 22, 2004. http://news.bbc.co.uk/2/hi/entertainment/3588432.stm.

5. Peter Gay, *Modernism: The Lure of Heresy from Baudelaire to Beckett and Beyond* (London: Vintage, 2007), 30.

6. Friedrich Nietzsche cited in Michael Burleigh, *Earthly Powers: Religion and Politics in Europe from the Enlightenment to the Great War* (London: HarperCollins, 2005), 11.

7. David F. Wells, *God in the Wasteland: The Reality of Truth in a World of Fading Dreams* (Grand Rapids, MI: Eerdmans, 1994), 101.

8. Richard Tarnas, *The Passion of the Western Mind: Understanding the Ideas That Have Shaped Our World View* (London: Pimlico, 1991), 389.

9. Wells, *God in the Wasteland*, 101.

10. Friedrich Nietzsche cited in Stephen N. Williams, *The Shadow of the AntiChrist: Nietzsche's Critique of Christianity* (Grand Rapids, MI: Baker, 2006), 228.

11. Jack Kerouac, *On the Road* (London: Penguin, 1955), 108.

12. Ibid.

13. Ibid.

Chapter 8: The Sixties

1. Jack Kerouac, *Desolation Angels* (London: Flamingo, 1965), 351–52.

2. "The path less beaten." *Touchstone* http://www.touchstonemag.com/archives/article.php?id=18-08-014-c.

3. Callum G. Brown, *The Death of Christian Britain: Understanding Secularisation* 1800–2000 (New York: Routledge, 2009), 190.

4. Ibid.

Chapter 9: The California Self

1. Martin Robinson, *Sacred Places, Pilgrim Paths: An Anthology of Pilgrimage* (London: HarperCollins, 1997), 2.

2. Ibid.

3. Ibid.

4. Ibid.

5. Ibid.

6. Ibid.

7. Ibid.

8. Nathaniel West, *The Day of the Locust* (New York: Random House, 1939), Kindle Edition.

9. Ibid.

10. Ibid.

11. John F. Schumaker, *The Age of Insanity: Modernity and Mental Health* (Westport, CT: Greenwood, 2001), 16.

Chapter 10: Superflat

1. Hugh Mackay, *Advance Australia . . . Where?: How We've Changed, Why We've Changed and What Will Happen Next* (Sydney: Hachette, 2007), 3.

2. Ibid.

3. See Takashi Murakami, *Superflat* (Tokyo: Madora Shuppan, 2000).

4. Jack Kerouac, *On the Road* (London: Penguin, 1955), 154.

5. Ibid, 176.

6. Ibid.

7. Ibid.

8. Hubert Dreyfus and Sean Dorrance Kelly, *All Things Shining: Reading the Western Classics to Find Meaning in a Secular Age* (New York: Free Press, 2012), Kindle Edition.

9. Abraham Heschel, *God in Seach of Man: A Philosophy of Judaism* (New York: Farrar, Straus and Giroux, 1955).

10. "The Arena Culture." *New York Times*, December 30, 2010. http://www.nytimes.com/2010/12/31/opinion/31brooks.html?_r=1.

Chapter 11: Feelings vs. Faith

1. See Sigmund Freud, *Civilization and Its Discontents*.

2. Craig M. Gay, *The Way of the (Modern) World: Or, Why It's Tempting to Live As If God Doesn't Exist* (Grand Rapids, MI: Eerdmans, 1998), 185.

3. Ibid.

4. Richard Sennett, *The Fall of Public Man* (London: Penguin, 1974), Kindle Edition.

5. Ibid.

6. Ibid.

7. Charles Taylor, *A Secular Age* (Cambridge, MA: Harvard University Press, 2007), 595.

Chapter 12: The Slavery of Absolute Freedom

1. See Clotaire Rapaille, *The Culture Code: An Ingenious Way to Understand Why People Around the World Live and Buy as They Do* (New York: Crown Business, 2007).

2. Katie Mills, *The Road Story and the Rebel: Moving Through Film, Fiction and Television* (Carbondale, IL: Southern Illinois University Press, 2006).

3. Barry Schwartz, *The Paradox of Choice: Why More Is Less* (New York: HarperCollins, 2004), 4.

4. See Isaiah Berlin, *Four Essays on Liberty* (New York: Oxford University Press USA, 1990).

5. Jonathan Franzen, *Freedom: A Novel* (New York: Farrar, Straus and Giroux, 2010), Kindle Edition.

6. Ibid.

7. Jean Twenge, *Generation Me: Why Today's Young Americans Are More Confident, Assertive, Entitled—and More Miserable Than Ever Before* (New York: Free Press, 2006), 21.

8. Robert N. Bellah, Richard Madsen, William M. Sullivan, Ann Swidler, and Steven M.Tipton, *Habits of the Heart: Individualism and Commitment in American Life* (Berkeley, CA: University of California Press, 1985).

Chapter 13: Faith on the Road

1. John Leleand, *Why Kerouac Matters: The Lessons of On the Road (They're Not What You Think)* (NewYork: Viking Press, 2007), 151.

2. Martin Robinson, *The Faith of the Unbeliever: Building Innovative Relationships with the Unchurched* (Crowborough, UK: Monarch, 1994), 87.

3. Brett McCracken, *Christian Hipsters: When Church and Cool Collide,* (Grand Rapids, MI, Baker, 2010), Kindle Edition.

4. Christian Smith and Melinda Lundquist Denton, *Soul Searching: The Religions and Spiritual Lives of American Teenagers* (New York: Oxford University Press, 2005), 162–63.

5. Ibid.

6. See Philip Jenkins, *God's Continent: Christianity, Islam, and Europe's Religious Crisis* (New York: Oxford University Press USA, 2009).

7. Tom Frame, *Losing My Religion: Unbelief in Australia* (Sydney: University of New South Wales Press, 2009), 190.

8. Ibid.

9. Hubert Dreyfus and Sean Dorrance Kelly, *All Things Shining: Reading the Western Classics to Find Meaning in a Secular Age* (New York: Free Press, 2012), Kindle Edition.

10. John Steinbeck, *East of Eden* (London: Penguin, 1992), Kindle Edition.

11. Jack Kerouac, *On the Road* (London: Penguin, 1955), 108.

Chapter 14: The Road Turns Into A Nightmare

1. Daniel Boorstin, *The Image; A Guide to Pseudo-Events in America* (New York: Vintage, 1961).

2. Ibid., 8.

3. Nathaniel West, *The Day of the Locust* (New York: Random House, 1939), Lindle Edition.

4. Ibid.

5. Chris Hedges. *Empire of Illusion: The End of Literacy and the Triumph of Spectacle* (New York: Nation Books, 2009), 52.

6. Ibid.

7. John Ralston Saul, *Voltaire's Bastards: The Dictatorship of Reason in the West* (New York: Vintage, 1993), 460.

8. Jack Kerouac, *On the Road* (London: Penguin, 1955), 236.

9. Author's notes from Amy Hungerford's lecture on *On the Road* at Yale University.

10. Kerouac, *On the Road*, 33.

11. Kerouac, *On the Road*, 49.

Chapter 15: At the End of the Road a Cross

1. Jack Kerouac, *Big Sur* (New York: HarperPerennial, 1966), 10.

2. Ibid.

3. Ibid.

4. Ibid., 156.

5. Ibid.

6. Ibid., 157.

7. Ibid., 164.

8. Ibid., 165.

9. Ben Giamo, *Kerouac, the Word and the Way: Prose Artist As Spiritual Quester* (Carbondale, IL: Southern Illinois University Press, 2000), 198.

10. Cited in Ellis Amburn, *Subterranean Kerouac: The Hidden Life of Jack Kerouac* (New York: St. Martin's Press, 1998), 373.

11. Jack Kerouac cited in Robert Inchausti, *Subversive Orthodoxy: Outlaws, Revolutionaries, and Other Christians in Disguise* (Grand Rapids, MI: Brazos, 2005), 73.

Chapter 16: The Road Home

1. Cormac McCarthy, *The Road* (New York: Vintage Books, 2006), 286.

2. Mark Sayers, "Looking under the Surface of the Millennial Generation," *Christian Research Journal*, 34–01 (2011).

Chapter 17: An Old Kind of Christian

1. 1 Corinthians 15:45.

2. Genesis 3:6.

Chapter 18: Leaving Ur

1. Ken Goffman, *Counter Culture through the Ages* (New York: Villard, 2005), 13.

2. Genesis 12:1.

3. Genesis 13:10.

4. Mark 1:13.

5. Revelation 21:2–4.

Chapter 19: Breaking Into Heaven

1. Thomas Cahill, *The Gift of the Jews: How a Tribe of Desert Nomads Changed the Way Everyone Thinks and Feels* (New York: Doubleday, 1998), 24.

2. Genesis 11:31.

3. Genesis 12:5.

4. Genesis 11:1–3.

5. Lewis Mumford, *The City in History: Its Origins, Its Transformations, and Its Prospects* (London: Secker & Warburg, 1961), 7.

6. See Ernest Becker, *The Denial of Death* (New York: Simon and Schuster, 1997).

7. Leon R. Kass, *The Beginning of Wisdom: Reading Genesis* (Chicago: Chicago University Press, 2003), 230.

8. Ibid.

9. Ibid.

10. R. R. Reno, *Genesis. Brazos Theological Commentary on the Bible* (Grand Rapids, MI: Brazos, 2010).

11. Kass, *The Beginning of Wisdom,* 232.

12. Jacques Ellul, *The Meaning of the City* (Grand Rapids, MI: Eerdmans, 1970).

13. Genesis 11:4.

14. Jonathan Sacks, *Covenant and Conversation: Genesis: The Book of Beginnings* (Jerusalem: Maggid, 2009).

Chapter 20: How Getting God Right Changes Everything

1. Richard Keyes in *No God but God: Breaking with the Idols of Our Age,* eds. Os Guinness and John Seel (Chicago: Moody. 1992), 38.

2. Allen Ginsberg, *Howl.*

3. Leviticus 20:2–5.

4. Barbara Ehrenreich, *Smile or Die: How Positive Thinking Fooled America and the World* (London: Granata, 2009), 140.

5. Ibid., 146.

Chapter 21: Holy Vandalism

1. http://www.compass.org.nz/conversations/2009/06/the-shack-a-review-part-3/.

2. *Relevant* Magazine, September/October, 65.

3. Christian Smith and Melinda Lundquist Denton, *Soul Searching: The Religions and Spiritual Lives of American Teenagers* (New York: Oxford University Press, 2005), 156.

4. Czeslaw Milosz, "The Discreet Charm of Nihilism." http://www.nybooks.com/articles/archives/1998/nov/19/discreet-charm-of-nihilism/.

5. William Dalrymple, *From the Holy Mountain: A Journey in the Shadow of Byzantium* (London: Harper Perennial, 1997), 251.

6. Revelation 1:12–16.

7. Joseph Mangina, *Revelation Brazos Theological Commentary on the Bible* (Grand Rapids, MI: Brazos Press, 2010), 49.

8. Revelation 4:6–8, 11.

Chapter 23: The Relationship That Changes the World

1. See Douglas Coupland, *Generation X: Tales of an Accelerated Culture* (New York: St. Martin's Griffin, 1991).

2. Genesis 17:1–7.

3. Shmuley Boteach, *Renewal: A Guide to the Values-Filled Life* (New York: Basic Books, 2010), Kindle Edition.

4. Philip Yancey, *Rumors of Another World: What on Earth Are We Missing?* (Grand Rapids, MI: Zondervan, 2003), 68.

5. Philip Rieff, *The Triumph of the Therapeutic: Uses of Faith after Freud* (New York: Harper Torchbooks, 1966).

6. John F. Kavanaugh, *Following Christ in a Consumer Society: The Spirituality of Cultural Resistance* (Maryknoll, NY: Orbis, 2004), 155.

7. Ibid.,

8. Genesis 17:9–13.

Chapter 24: Cultivating Creation

1. Samuel Taylor Coleridge, "Ode to Dejection."

2. Aidan Day, *Romanticism: The New Critical Idiom* (London: Routledge, 1996), Kindle Edition chapter 2.

3. Giles Milton, *Nathaniel's Nutmeg: Or, the True and Incredible Adventures of the Spice Trader Who Change the Course of History* (New York: Farrar, Straus and Giroux, 1999).

4. Jack Turner, *Spice: The History of a Temptation* (London: Harper Perennial, 2004), xxvii.

5. Psalm 19:1–4.

6. G. K. Chesterton, *Orthodoxy* (Peabody, MA: Hendricksons, 2006), 2⁵

7. Ibid.

8. Michael W. Goheen and Craig G. Bartholomew, *Living at the Crossroad: An Introduction to Christian Worldview* (Grand Rapids, MI: Baker, 2008), Kindle Edition.

9. Genesis 15:9–17 TNIV.

Chapter 25: Finding Hope in an Atomic Holocaust

1. I consulted a number of sources for the background for this chapter. The most accessible and moving account was Paul Glynn, *A Song for Nagasaki: The Story of Takashi Nagai—Scientist, Convert, and Survivor of the Atomic Bomb* (San Francisco CA: Ignatius Press, 2009). Also helpful was the essay in Robert Ellsberg, *All Saints: Daily Reflections on Saints, Prophets, and Witnesses for Our Time* (New York: Crossroad, 1997), 12. See also Paul Ham, *Hiroshima Nagasaki* (Sydney: Harper Collins, 2011).

2. You can easily find on YouTube the clip of Oppenheimer recounting his words. The footage is quite incredible, the pain on his face speaks volumes.

3. Luke 17:10.

4. Stephen Fry made this comment during a public conversation with Christopher Hitchens at the 2005 Hay Arts and Literature Festival in Wales.

5. David Kinnaman, *You Lost Me: Why Young Christians Are Leaving Church . . . And Rethinking Faith* (Grand Rapids, MI: Baker, 2011), Kindle Edition.

6. "Auguries of Innocence" *in William Blake: Selected Poems* (Oxford, UK: Oxford University Press, 1996), 173.

INCITING INCIDENTS

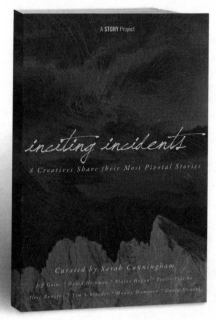

978-0-8024-0624-8

Inciting Incidents combines unique stories from eight creatives (artists, musicians, writers, thinkers, and leaders) managing the tensions between their faith, their place in life, and their work as artists. By capturing this next generation's battle between idealism and reality, these storytellers create understanding of those moments that truly shape us. Readers will be challenged to use their own art and their own life stories to find their way in God's kingdom. The end result is that God has created each of us uniquely and we each have a growing part to play in His story.

MOODY
PUBLISHERS
www.MoodyPublishers.com